Sacred Strands

Sermons by Minnesota Women

Barbara Mraz, Editor

Drawings by Susan S. Friesen

Preface

Strange how life is a circle. The plea of my adolescence was "Let me out of the church!" The plea of my mid-life is, "Let me back in...." No deeper than that, for I could have come back at any time, and I have and left again. My plea now is, "Let this have meaning. Let this have the meaning I need it to have."

My first memories are of church and a tiny parsonage in Leaf River, Illinois, the year my father interned in a rural Methodist parish. My father preached. My mother played the piano. And I learned to be very, very good. My father's voice from the pulpit had the family cadence that all the ordained Baldwins have. His voice could have been my grandfather, my Uncle Don, my cousin Donald, my cousin George, my cousin Roy. It could have been myself, the summer I was 12, struck with inspiration along the shores of church camp, thinking about the ministry, wanting to take my place. The camp chaplain indulged me for a week before explaining that women could not be ordained. Women are ordained now, and their voices are the ringing bells that call me back to my tradition.

Visiting Episcopal parishes in 1988-89, I realize I have come for the body and the blood. Sitting through the liturgy, then strange after years when a silent circle or the natural world was my worship, I wait for the sacrament to be offered. I have tasted this moment before, but never fully taken and never deeply received.... I have come to test my readiness again, mine and the church's, our ability to meet at the rail. I weave moments of private prayer into the flow of words. I kneel when they kneel. It is kneeling I have come for too. My body folds into this posture with relief, though I have not prayed much on my knees. Prayed sitting. Prayed cross-legged. Prayed on the run. Kneeling feels like the position I need to assume for the next conversation I want to have with God.

And the conversation I want to have is whether or not

God will unsex himself enough from this tradition, so that I can sit here and find a translation of Christianity that will communicate to me, and allow me to communicate back. I know that God and can speak...the question is: can we speak in church?

My previous congregation was Quaker Meeting, and I haven't gone for years. I built an amalgam of spiritual tradition: yoga and meditation, native American rituals, long dog rambles in the countryside, baptismal boat rides, pilgrimages to the ocean. I avoided where I came from and Sunday morning became a time sacred for its quietness, a hole in the week when I would not be disturbed. Now I have started to disturb it, to dress and head out the door in search of something I cannot explain - a woman seeking the sacraments, in need of wine and bread.

I'm here. I'm trying. I open my mouth in this Episcopal church on a Sunday morning nearly forty years after the Leaf River parsonage and try to follow the strange melodic lines of different hymns, the sung responses of the Eucharist. I flip through the prayerbook a little madly, looking for the right page. It doesn't matter. It only means that I am new. It does not interfere with my questions or my quest.

Eucharist is prepared, sung to, spoken about, the elements lifted. I approach the rail, kneel, hold out my hands. "Body of Christ given for you...." My head snaps up. This is a woman's voice. I feel the soft tip of her slender fingers place the bread in the palm of my hand. At her shoulder, another woman holds the cup, I take it, carefully to my lips. She says, "Blood of Christ the cup of salvation." Woman to woman we pass the body. We pass the blood. Two thousand years of pronouns disappear. Two thousand years of exclusion fall away. I transcend the language and recognize the ritual. It lies sweet on my tongue.

I have not become ordained, but my sisters have. They carry my voice to the altar, and speak my quest from the pulpit. They feed me food and give me space where I can explore a woman's sense of place and tradition, and break new spiritual territory.

Christina Baldwin, author two premier books on journal-writing: _One to One_ (M. Evans and Co., 1977), and _Life's Companion_ (Bantam, 1991).

Contents

Introduction

"I told him that I had been at a meeting that morning of the people called Quakers, when I had heard a woman preaching. He replied, 'Sir, a woman preaching is like a dog walking on his hind legs. It is not done well; but you are surprised to find it done at all." James Boswell, *Life of Samuel Johnson*, 1763

Why a book of *sermons*?

Why a book of sermons *by women*?

Because they're good reading, ask you to think about some of life's tougher questions, and celebrate the work of a group of people who are still, in some ways, a curiosity.

This book is a celebration of the work being done by women clergy throughout Minnesota. It is interdenominational in content, ecumenical in spirit, and welcomes men and women as its readers.

In *Sacred Strands* you will meet eight Minnesota clergywomen of varying backgrounds, ages, and religious traditions. Some have been in the ministry only a year or two, others considerably longer. One is on a staff of eight pastors at a Twin Cities "mega-church" of thirteen thousand members. Another is pastor of a small rural church where her Sunday duties include not only preaching the sermon but also starting the furnace. Two are rabbis. Another is co-minister at a church with her husband. Some have grown children; one has a baby only weeks old. Some entered divinity or rabbinical school right after college; for others this came after raising a family. And the initial expectation of one is for a profession with "no math and no sex." Each woman shares part of her story - as well as two of her sermons - on these pages. The women included in this collection are known as good preachers. Each considers preaching a key element, not only of her ministry but also of her spirituality.

The sermons are diverse in approach and in emphasis.

5

Some are personal narratives or reflections, some are based on Biblical events, others employ poetic structures or make strong theological statements. There are sermons here that were delivered on holidays - Mother's Day, Christmas, Purim, Thanksgiving - as well as at regular weekly services.

If there is one word to describe these sermons, it is to say that they are *accessible*. These are not the sermons of old which began with clear-cut conclusions, admonitions and prescriptions for life, and then relied solely on the authority of the Church and of the minister for credibility, persuasion, and inspiration. Rather, the sermons in this book are about the everyday, the personal, the immediate, and those daily experiences and observations that have led to an understanding of who God is and how we should live. They are more inductive than deductive. In that sense they are traditionally "feminine."

Elizabeth Dodson Grey writes:

Instead of distancing ourselves and withdrawing from the reality of life to find sacredness, we go toward that reality - towards bodies, towards nature, toward food, toward dust, toward transitory moments in relationship. And wherever we look, we find that which nourishes us and deepens us.

And so there are sermons here that are illuminated with memories - of childhood friends, of decorating the house for the holidays, of childbirth and parenting, of lunches with friends. But these down-to-earth illustrations support profound scriptural and theological themes that are central to the faith of each woman. In the Yale Lectures on Preaching in 1877, Phillips Brooks, known in his time as "the prince of preachers," observed that "The preachers that have moved and held men have always preached doctrine. No exhortation to a good life that does not put behind it some truth as deep as eternity can seize and hold the conscience."

An interesting sidelight is that an inductive style of

preaching is increasingly recognized as effective with the contemporary audience. As listeners have been affected by the general disrespect for authority of all types that has defined America in the Seventies and Eighties, a heavy-handed, authoritarian style of preaching has become less effective than ever. In *As One Without Authority*, Fred B. Craddock, professor of homiletics at Candler School of Theology in Atlanta, endorses sermons in which "thought moves from the particulars of experience that have a familiar ring in the listener's ear to a general truth or conclusion." He suggests that this method "respects rather than insults the hearer and it leaves him the freedom and hence the obligation to respond." This style of preaching predominates in this collection.

Some aspects of this book are unusual. A sermon is written to be spoken, yet these will be read. Factors of delivery and vocal expression cannot be conveyed on the printed page, so we have selected sermons that read well. And although sermons are *oral* communication, we have chosen to bring in a *visual* dimension through artwork. We also wanted to convey a serious purpose in the title, so some titles we abandoned with reluctance. They were fun, but risked trivializing the material (some favorites: *Pearls in the Pulpit, Date with an Angel*). Also, giving the collection the diversity and ecumenical balance we wanted was a challenge.

Special thanks to all those women who submitted sermons, to those not represented on these pages who have endorsed the importance of this venture in countless ways, to my husband Steve Bougie for endless hours of listening and encouragement, to my daughters Anna and Emily for reminding me to lighten up, to Judi Brandt for the idea for this collection, and to the Lois Granner Fund for Christian Education of the Episcopal Diocese of Minnesota, who allowed this project its beginning.

Barbara Mraz

To all those women who have been "the first"
the daughters who follow
and those men who have the courage
to walk with them ...

Rev. Kristine M. Holmgren

The Rev. Kristine M. Holmgren

Born: St. Paul, Mn..

Religious Background: A religious smorgasbord: baptized Presbyterian, raised in the Evangelical and Reformed Church, confirmed United Church of Christ, rediscovered Presbyterianism in 1970 and ordained Presbyterian in 1979.

Educational Background: Creative Writing Program, University of California, 1971; B.A. With Honors in Religious Studies, Macalester College, 1975; M. Div., Princeton Theological Seminary, 1979.

Professional Activity: Pastor of Laurel Presbyterian Church of Hager City, Wisconsin, since June, 1986. Duties ("You name it...I'll do it!") include sweeping the sanctuary, writing and printing the bulletins, turning on the furnace Sunday mornings, preaching, baptizing, teaching confirmation and adult education, burying the dead, leading a creative and imaginative youth group; formerly Chaplain of Macalester College, (1977-1979); Associate Pastor of First Presbyterian of South St. Paul, (1979-1982); Director of the Youth Advisory Council of Northfield (1982-1985); Salvation Army of Philadelphia (1976-1977); youth worker at Grace Cathedral in San Francisco (1969-1971).

Personal: Married to Gary B. Deason, Assoc. Professor of History, Religion & Philosophy at College of St. Olaf; two children, Grace Margaret, age nine, Claire Bernice, age seven.

Interests and hobbies: Swimming, knitting, playing with my children; teaching creative writing to young people and adults; teaching knitting to children; creative and freelance writing (frequent contributor to the *Star-Tribune, Minnesota Calls, Horizons, Lutheran Woman Today*; novel in progress).

I performed my first wedding when I was six years old.

It was in the summer of 1955. My older brother John and I set up a church in the ravine near our house and set about bringing in the faithful. He was supposed to be the minister. But when he found out what ministers wore, he said it was too "sissy" and backed out. So I put on my mother's bath robe and conducted our first worship service in the elms by the railroad tracks on Dunlap Avenue in St. Paul.

News of the church traveled fast.

It wasn't long before several of our playmates wanted me to marry them. It was a solemn moment when Stevie Schechter placed the cigar band ring on Kathy McDonald's finger and said, "With this ring, I thee wed." But when I pronounced them man and wife, Stevie did not want to kiss the bride. So I kissed them both. That was my first wedding.

There were many funerals in those days. Dead birds were everywhere. I said tender words over maggot-filled squirrels that other clergy would have ignored. John found the cigar boxes and did the dirty work. All I had to do was talk about life eternal and close with the Lord's prayer. The work seemed pleasant enough. I decided to become a minister when I grew up.

It must have been the right decision. My parishioners seem to enjoy the stories I tell from their pine pulpit. They are quick to invite me home for a bowl of Sunday soup and a ham sandwich. They are hard working, stubborn people with an independence that frightened some of their previous ministers. For a reason that only God knows, they have invited me into their lives. I am there at times when they need to give up their strength. They are precious to me. They are my family of faith. The first I have known.

My parents weren't church going people. I was one of those kids dropped off at the front door for Sunday school and picked up after service. A person doesn't get over that experience easily.

I remember when Rev. Schmeichen visited my parents, encouraging them to attend worship. But there wasn't much anyone could do to get my father out of his pajamas on Sunday morning, or my mother squeezed into a girdle for Summit Avenue church going.

There was some hope that John would go into the ministry. He was such a quiet, studious boy. Rev. Schmeichen would pat my brother's knee, look my father in the eye and say what a fine, young Christian boy we had.

But I was all that Rev. Schmeichen could shake loose from the Holmgren family. I'm certain he never dreamed that the little girl with the smart mouth would go through with her threat to be a minister.

Because of my upbringing, I was never an "insider" in the church. Even now, I sometimes feel like someone peeking in the windows of the institution, wondering if I belong. That is probably why I love to preach. In the pulpit I don't concern myself with the pettiness of whether I am in the right place at the right time.

Instead, I merely listen for the prayers of the people. As I lead them in the singing of their hymns, I am surrounded by the magic I discovered with my ravine playmates in the summer of 1955. I remember the summer sun, warming us as we sang "Sweet Hour of Prayer." My mother's ragged chenille robe, wrapped around a tee shirt and jeans remains the most comfortable vestment I have ever worn.

God has called me to a simple ministry. I don't look for much more than what I have already received. My expectations are modest. When I was ordained, all I anticipated was a profession with no math and no sex. So far, I haven't been disappointed.

The Rev. Kristine M. Holmgren
Laurel Presbyterian Church, Hager City, Wisconsin
February 28, 1988

A Death in the Neighborhood

>*"For those who want to save their life will lose it, and those who lose their life for my sake and for the sake of the gospel, will save it. For what does it profit them to gain the whole world and forfeit their soul? Indeed, what can they give in return for their soul?" -Mark :35-37*

When I was a little girl growing up on Goodrich Avenue in St. Paul, there was a family in our neighborhood with little money and lots of children. They were the Fletchers and they had a little girl my age named Christine. We had the same first name, we both lived on Goodrich Avenue and we loved to roller skate. But similarities ended there.

The Fletchers were Catholic and we were some kind of Protestant. Christine's father was an alcoholic. Mine was a Mason. There were twelve children in her family and two in mine. Christine was a middle child, lost between six or seven older and younger siblings. I was the cherished baby in my home.

As a child, it seemed to me that the Fletcher family struggled every day of their life. I never saw Mrs. Fletcher smile, or stop to chat with the other mothers. Her husband didn't mow the lawn like our fathers did. Instead, two or three times in the summer, one of the children, thin and dirty, pushed a rusty mower across their overgrown, weeded lot. The Fletcher kids spent most of the winter outdoors, barely dressed. They played in the snow with socks to cover their feet. When the socks were too wet they headed indoors for dry socks and came out to play again.

The family kept to themselves. When their father was drinking he became a mean drunk. On winter evenings the neighborhood would be filled with muffled screams from the Fletcher home as he beat his children.

When the storm windows came off the Fletcher house in the spring, the cries of children cut through the neighborhood like razors. It sliced us away from our play and paralyzed us, turning our eyes toward the brick house where some unmentionable torture occurred. Our parents would not talk about the Fletcher family. But we knew that the Fletcher children suffered. No one could hide the anger of that house from us.

I did not want to play with Christine Fletcher. I could have, I guess, but I had no reason to. She always looked tired, sick. I didn't think she would enjoy a day skating in the sunshine as I did.

But one summer afternoon when I was eight years old, my mother invited Chrissy Fletcher to our house for lemonade.

I came out of the house in my roller skates. Chrissy had hers too, and was sitting with my mother in our father-built glider swing in the back yard. My mother made lemonade with mint from the garden and a fresh batch of chocolate chip cookies. Chrissy sat next to her and talked non-stop.

I joined them on the swing as one story led into another. Chrissy said she liked the nun who was going to be her teacher at St. Luke's next year and she was excited about the skates that her sister Audrey had outgrown. They would belong to her in August. "I can skate in style all through third grade," Christine said.

Then, the strangest thing happened. My mother's chin quivered as it does on Mother's Day after she opens her card from my father. Her eyes misted over and she turned from us, retreating into her kitchen.

Christine and I studied each other for a moment. Then,

when I shrugged off my mother's odd behavior she asked, "Do you like war movies?"

I didn't. I preferred old Shirley Temple films on WCCO. But I knew that most eight-year-old girls thought Shirley was a joke.

"Yes," I lied. "I love war movies."

"Do you like Audie Murphy?"

I had no idea who Audie Murphy was. But Christine knew. He was a dream-boat movie star, she said. He had a baby face and he was a famous Nazi killer. She recited the names of the movies he made as she bent to tighten her roller skates.

That was when I noticed it. It began somewhere between her shoulders and spread to the base of her neck, twisting her spine, pressing against her tee shirt. Christine had a hump on her back. I didn't know that young backs could grow gnarled and bent.

When Christine rose from tightening her skates, her eyes were bright with the telling of one of Audie's famous suicide runs. I noticed her posture for the first time. She was not straight like the rest of my friends but bent, like an old woman.

We left the back yard and started skating the jagged sidewalk that laced Goodrich Avenue. Christine, for all her smiles and enthusiasm, was in pain. She tripped many times on the uneven cement, falling on scabbed knees. But she refused to end our day by going home. We played until the street lights came on. Finally, my mother's strong voice called me to dinner. I left Christine smiling and waving to me from the corner near her house. It was the only time we ever played together.

Later, mother told me how Christine complained to her own mother about pains in her back.

"She's trying to take me away from the babies," her mother told mine. When she continued to say she hurt, her mother took her to the hospital, "to frighten the truth back

15

into her." Later, when my mother told the story she said that Mrs. Fletcher's face never revealed a thing when she found out the truth from the doctor. Chrissy had cancer.

The city poured new concrete on our avenue in July. They took out the ragged blocks that tripped us in our skating. In their place they put white slabs of concrete, a skater's dream. There were signs posted all over the neighborhood warning us to respect the newly poured sidewalks along Goodrich Avenue.

One sticky hot evening after the cement workers left, my mother and I were sitting on the front porch swing reading when Christine came to examine the new sidewalk. She was thin, pale and no longer resembled a child. Her long red hair hung in neglected knots down her gnarled back. She wrapped a narrow arm around the shoulders of her older sister, Audrey, who helped her walk.

I saw her do it. Ignoring the workman's signs, Christine walked across the wet cement in her bare feet. Then, on her knees, I saw her autograph her vandalism. She laughed when Audrey helped her stand. Then, putting her hands on hips, she turned toward our house and stuck her tongue out at me. She was still a defiant little Fletcher, in spite of her pain. I smiled at her and waved.

She died in August. My mother said I was too young to go to the funeral. So the day of the mass of the angels passed without notice in my house. Christine was gone. There was one less ragamuffin in the neighborhood.

Two years later the Fletchers moved to California. It seemed to me that everyone forgot her.

But every summer, when I found a barefoot afternoon, I walked to the block of cement where Christine placed her feet. For years I could place mine in hers, the fit being nearly perfect. Then mine began to overtake all ten of her little prints.

Those summer moments were heavy with a reverence that was new to me as I stood on the sidewalk and thought of all the snowballs I had thrown that year. I thought of the hot dogs I had eaten, all of the lessons at the YWCA. I remembered the 4th of July fireworks and the frozen toes of January sleigh rides that I had endured. I thought of how much of life Christine missed. She was dead. Everything ended for her. But I was still alive.

I began to dream of death, of the end of all things I knew. Someday my mother and father would die. Someday I would die, too.

Perhaps I would live to be ten, eleven years old. Perhaps I would live to be seventy-five or eighty. But it mattered little. The reality was death. It knew no boundaries. If an eight year old child was dead and forgotten, so could we all be.

With death a reality, the meaning of life became important to me. What was the purpose of existence? Why do some children survive to adulthood and others suffer with bent bodies and die?

Of course, I did not know that these were questions that confront all of us. I did not know that humanity had been dealing with these questions since the age of reason. I thought these were original concerns. It would be years before I would know that these were heady thoughts for an eight year old. I didn't know that grown men and women crumble before these questions.

But I knew that Chrissy had not crumbled. My proof was in the foot prints. There, in front of my house, supported by her sister, Chrissy dared to place herself in my life forever.

None of us can escape the truth of the reality of death. Every person needs to look straight into the face of death and ask the hard questions of life. Christine did that. As she stepped into the cement, she also stepped into the collective memory of my neighborhood. Because she refused to go away quietly, we could not hide from the cruelty of her life and the insanity of her death. Like all things evil, we must face them as imprinted always on our reality, just as we affirm the beauty of a bright summer day.

Last summer I took my children to visit their grandmother on Goodrich Avenue. She still lives in the same place. The sidewalk with Christine's footprints are still near her front porch.

When we arrived, my children disappeared to play outdoors. Soon my six year old daughter found Christine's foot prints in the cement.

"Momma," she called from the front yard. My mother and I went to join her. "Look at these little foot prints," she said. "My feet fit these feet." She removed her shoes and placed her tiny feet into the cement where Christine stood thirty years before. I felt my heart open, wide and full. The ghost of Christine washed over me. She came to me, frail and defiant. Again I saw her, leaning against her sister, hands on her hips, sticking her tongue out at the world.

My daughter's pink toes wiggled to meet Christine's dimensions. "My feet are almost like these," she said.

Almost, I thought. But Christine's childhood was not seasoned with ballet lessons, zoo trips and dreams of Disney World.

God gives to all the great gift of life. The truth is that some lives are more treasured than others. Some children are born, it seems, to suffer and die. But Christ promises us that innocence and love are stronger than abuse or neglect. Christ promises that those who lose their lives for the sake of the gospel will not lose their souls.

Innocence and love are virtues that may appear as frail as a sick child. They may seem weak and helpless attributes. But they are stronger than the most powerful blows that are brought against them.

Chrissy Fletcher was a brave little girl. When she waved at me from the wet cement, she taught me that life is an extraordinary blessing. Even in the tough times, there are opportunities for story telling and back yard lemonade made by someone else's mother. When life is merely a stop-over to death, there is still time for a secret love for a war-hero movie star. The human spirit can be leeched by cruelty or neglect. But it may also triumph with a defiance born of joy and innocence.

Chrissy taught me that none of us get through life without suffering. But we can always find a friend who will stay with us until darkness falls and the sound of a gentle voice calls us home.

Drawing by Susan Friesen

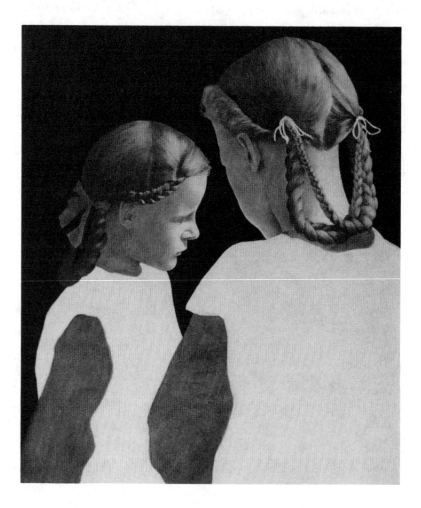

The Rev. Kristine M. Holmgren
First United Church of Christ, Northfield, Minnesota
December 4, 1983

The Meek and Mild Myth

"My soul magnifies the Lord, and my spirit rejoices in God, my Savior, for he has looked with favor on the lowliness of his servant, Surely, from now on, all generations will call me blessed!" Luke 1: 46-47

One of my favorite parts of Advent is decorating the house for the holiday. Just like you, I have a little manger scene with all the principals in appropriate poses and attire. Joseph is bearded and wise, kneeling on one knee with his eyes wide and adoring. There are a variety of angels, dangerously bold in their white wings and silver gowns. Their faces are painted in placid splendor, smiles that anticipate the coming of the wonderful holiday.

Then, I unpack the quiet queen of the pageant. My little Mary is like all the other Marys in all the manger scenes under all the Christmas trees in Minnesota. Dressed in blue, head covered with a quiet veil and cocked to one side, her humility is painful. Her tiny hands are pressed together in prayer. She looks appropriately meek, mild.

When I was a little girl in church school we had a church pageant every year. We started planning at Thanksgiving. The Saturday following, all the children from Sunday School met in the sanctuary to be assigned their parts by the minister's wife, Mrs. Schmeichen. She did most of the organizing, and our mothers sewed the costumes. But the props I loved were right there in the church, hidden all year by our ingenious sexton and then revealed on that glorious Saturday.

Today, thirty years later, I still get goose bumps when I

remember Rev. Schmeichen and the Deacons as they unwrapped those extravagant props. There was a tremendous cardboard star sprayed with gold and hanging from black string. There was a wooden manger with real straw and shepherd crooks carved from pine. The cattle and sheep were made from chicken wire and paper mache and were as big as real cattle.

For me, the most magical part of the Christmas pageant was the large blue light bulb that was invisibly hooked to the center of the manger. It threw a cool, azure glow that was supposed to be the halo of the baby Jesus. The effect was spellbinding. The blue light washed the person of Mary in the magic of Christmas. The girl who played Mary would sit in the spotlight of its glow, meek, demure, sweet. She was dressed in the same unbelievably lovely gown every year. It was made of blue velvet, soft and dignified.

The year that I was in fifth grade, I went to the pageant meeting convinced that I would be chosen as Mary. Why shouldn't I be Mary? I was the smartest girl in Sunday School. I knew the Ten Commandments by heart in third grade. I was the first girl in my class to memorize the beatitudes. Why shouldn't it be me? Besides, I was ready. I had my acceptance speech ready in my head.

"Why, this is so unexpected," I would say to Mrs. Schmeichen.

"Surely, you don't mean it?" Mrs Schmeichen would be shocked at my modesty. "Why, you are the only choice! Who else could possibly communicate the composure, the poise..."

Needless to say, I thought I had it made.

But fantasy and reality seldom cooperate. Mrs. Schmeichen, gray hair tucked neatly in a bun at the base of her stocky neck, smiled her twinkling grin at all of us. Then, turning toward Marilyn Perkins' mother, she said, "Now we need a nice, quiet little girl with dark hair and dark eyes to play Mary."

Scanning our eager pale faces in the pews, she looked past my blonde head, as though she was looking for someone else. Was she expecting Patty Duke to bounce into the sanctuary, released from Metro-Goldwyn for the role? And what's this thing about dark hair, I thought? Patty had a previous engagement, but I was ready!

Then, Mrs. Schmeichen's eyes landed on the only brunette in our church, sweet Marilyn Perkins. With an artificial look of surprise, Mrs. Schmeichen said what she said last year, and the year before that.

"Marilyn! Of course. Marilyn it is then."

Marilyn...who didn't know the words to the Lord's Prayer. Marilyn...a swarthy, quiet little girl with brown eyes and a father who was Chairman of the Church Council. Marilyn was Mary every year. I was issued another set of wings and robes.

So, on Christmas Eve, I reluctantly joined the long line of other Nordic types as we crooned, "Angels From the Realms of Glory."

I made the most of it. I threw a kiss to the audience, like Dinah Shore did when she wanted all of us to see the U.S.A. in a Chevrolet. But while I was hamming it up in the chorus, Marilyn Perkins was sitting quietly, peacefully, gazing with sweet repose at the glorious blue light bulb that was the baby Jesus. Marilyn Perkins. Meek and mild. Just like the real thing. Just like Mary.

I was never easy with the concept. As I grew older and studied scripture, the image of the little blue Mary began to trouble me in new ways.

I learned that Mary was a first century Jewish woman. I also learned what that meant. As such, Mary understood that a man owned his daughters, a husband owned his wife. A pious Jewish woman lived her entire life in the company of family and under the roof of her father, learning the ways of a Jewish wife. She left that home when she moved into the house of her new husband. She was not allowed to

23

walk the streets of her town alone; she was always veiled and accompanied by her father or by other women. No man spoke to her. She spoke to no man other than her father, husband or brother.

If, by some misfortune, she were to marry and not bear male children, her husband had the right by law to reject her through divorce. If she was divorced by her husband, she had two choices: starvation because of the ostracism, or joining the community of outcast women ... the prostitutes.

Mary knew these laws. They were ardently enforced by the Pharisees. She knew that her piety and purity were the most valuable parts of her humanity. Without them she would be cast out, humiliated and murdered by her own people. She was the daughter of Heli, a direct descendent of David. Mary knew that her adherence to Jewish law was important so that the lineage of David might be carried forth.

We can imagine her horror at hearing the words of the Angel Gabriel. A meek and mild woman would have shirked before the vision of the challenge from the Angel of God. But when we read the scripture we see that there is no horror in Mary's response. There is no fear. She merely says, "May it be to me as you have said." So, with these brave words of consent, Mary conceived the son of God.

Several years ago there was a special on television about the visitation of Mary and her consequential struggles with Joseph when he discovered that she was pregnant before they married. Mary was portrayed by Jane Seymour or some other gorgeous brunette. The actress played Mary as a person who trembled a great deal. Joseph and she took lots of long walks in the woods, giving the wind ample opportunity to blow her blue gown in graceful folds. Mary was portrayed as a meek woman, lovely because of her quiet and thoughtful acceptance of God's will.

But when I read scripture I can't find this Mary. When

I look at my Christmas cards with the Virgin solemn and head bowed, I don't see the Mary of scripture.

Mary was more to Jesus than a meek vessel who gave him life. She believed in him, understood his destiny. She alone, unlike any other disciple, was with him from the beginning to the end of his ministry.

She was with Jesus as he grew into Jewish manhood. While we know little of the childhood of Jesus, we do know that the customs and traditions appropriate for a first-century Jewish boy mandated the presence and continual instruction by the father and the nurturing love of a mother. Mary was there.

We have the story of Jesus' celebration of the Passover in his twelfth year, and the way in which Mary questioned him when he strayed from the family. We know that when Jesus responded to his mother's reprimand, Mary pondered his words in her heart. They were the first words Jesus said to claim authority in the temple. Mary was there.

We have the story of the wedding in Cana. We remember how Jesus changed the water to wine, revealing himself as the Messiah for the first time. Mary was there.

We remember the ways in which Jesus referred to his mother in his preaching, and how many times he mentioned his relationships to his family and his spiritual connections with the family of believers. Mary was there.

According to Acts, after Jesus' Ascension, Mary was with the disciples in the upper room. After that, we hear nothing more of Mary. Legend takes over. Some traditions say that she lived out the rest of her days with the beloved disciple John, as Jesus commanded her to do from the cross. Others say that her body is in the Tomb of the Virgin Mary in the Valley of Kidrin, but historical evidence does not support this theory. The Orthodox believe that she was assumed, body and soul, into heaven. Protestants reject this interpretation.

But one thing we all agree upon is this: Mary was

present with Jesus from the beginning to the end. Mary took the ministry of Jesus in its entirety, from those stirring moments of his childhood affirmation of his mission, to his baptism, his message from the Mount, to the gore of Golgatha. Mary was there, following, loving and caring for her son.

This was no meek and mild little woman. This was no praying, passive disciple. This was a woman of strength, will, and great faith. Mary, facing the angel Gabriel who gives her the terrible and challenging news that she will conceive as an unmarried woman, says, "Let it be to me as you have said." We all know that she followed this statement with the glorious praise of God found in the passage we call the Magnificat.

Mary accepted the will of God knowing that it would involve a life-long pilgrimage of joy and suffering, enthusiasm and depletion, heartbreak and unbelievable love. The scriptures tell us that Mary pondered the truths of Jesus' mission in her heart; a heart aggressively committed to doing the will of God, following Jesus that the weak might be exalted and the mighty overthrown. This was not a meek and mild woman.

And so, when I was invited to set up my first Christmas pageant in my first church, I chose the rowdiest, most irrepressible red head in the Sunday school to be my Mary. I dressed her in red and she danced with the angels. For I believed then, and I do now, that Mary danced that night as well. She knew, as we do, that God loved her, and chose her for a life that was rich and full. She knew then, as we know today, that God's love was most perfectly expressed in the love of a child for his mother, a woman of strength and great faith.

Mary has taught us great things. Not the least of these is that the power of God can reveal life in such fullness that there are no edges; only a rich and tender mercy.

Reverend Anna Carter Florence

The Rev. Anna Carter Florence

Born: Rochester, New York
Religious Background: Presbyterian
Education: B.A. History with Theater Studies, Yale, 1984;
M. Div. in New Testament Studies; Wailes Prize in New
Testament; Friar's Award, Princeton Seminary, 1988.
Employment: Associate Pastor, Westminster Presbyterian
Church, Minneapolis (youth and young adult ministries;
planning worship); internships in finance and in theater;
employment with UNICEF.
Personal: married to David Carter Florence (Presbyterian
pastor at Plymouth Congregational Church, Minneapolis);
Caleb Martin, born August 20, 1991.
Hobbies and Interests: theater, music, poetry,
needlework, our two dogs, puzzles, reading, swimming.

It wasn't the original plan. In fact, it wasn't even
among the back-up options. I suppose there might have
been clues all along, subtle patterns that an observant and
sensitive person might piece together in retrospect, but we
never noticed them, my family and I. For us, they were
simply stories of a vaguely humorous nature: the day my
brother and I served communion to a congregation of one
(our mother) in the upstairs playroom; the winter I refused
to go to Sunday school and chose instead to read the Pearl
S. Buck _Story Bible_ piled under blankets in the backseat of
our car; the year I played the angel Gabriel in the
Christmas pageant, and from my hiding place behind the
pulpit, stood up on the minister's seat throughout the
entire show so as not to miss any of the action. We would
never have looked at these events while they were
happening and said among ourselves, "Yes, it seems that
little Anna is destined to be a preacher."

What turns a person toward the ministry? Is it the
stories such as these, the rhythmic living out of days and
lives in the community of the church, or the cataclysmic

events that shake one to the very core? I have experienced some of both, and it seems to me that the rhythms must precede the earthquakes. Without the years I spent day-dreaming in worship and dawdling through Sunday school, without those countless Saturday mornings when I explored the crevices of the sanctuary while my mother arranged the flowers for the Sunday service, without the years in youth fellowships, and the days I sang quavering solos with my father from the balcony, I would have no foundation to shake. I grew up with the community of Christ in my veins and beneath my feet. This is what allowed me, in a fever of adolescent certainty, to throw it all out the window, and to muck about in alternative spiritualities as I experimented with shaking up my own foundations. But it is also what allowed me to realize that ultimately, God does the best foundation shaking, and eventually leads us back home to a familiar place.

So when people ask me how I became a minister, I have a hard time answering definitely. There are things I can point to - these stories, for example, and the fact that I come from a line of Presbyterian pastors, and the time I was travelling in India and felt an urgency to change directions and do some work beyond myself - but I know that these are sketchy details at best. I do not have a dramatic Damascus event to share, and perhaps that's best; I've never trusted things or people that are absolutely CERTAIN. I like ambiguity. It is the unfinished nature of the gospel that appeals to me. Even as I place my faith squarely within the grace of God, I treasure the fact that God throws curve balls at us when we are expecting straight lines and square edges.

I respond better when I am asked what I like about my work. I presently serve as an associate pastor at Westminster Presbyterian Church in Minneapolis. Westminster is a large downtown church in the old "cathedral church" tradition: Sunday worship services are central to our congregational life, even as we strive to become a place where vital ministry happens every day of the week. My responsibility is largely with youth and young adults. We spend our days together searching for a point of belonging somewhere on the spectrum of faith, a place where we feel we can be faithful to God and ourselves. Learning to live with God in mind is an incredible journey. It takes us through fellowship events and discussion nights, to leading worship for the congregation. The time I spend with our youth and young adults keeps me honest. They do not tolerate easy answers; they push me to make things relevant as well as true.

At Westminster, I have the opportunity to preach occasionally, and here I have found another journey of incredible proportions. My parents, a physician and a poet, taught me about the music of words, and about work my soul must have. Preaching has combined these two things for me. The act of exegeting a text and writing a sermon has become part of my blood, part of how I make sense of the world and the Word of God. When I begin, it is like taking up a script and starting to read through it without the benefit of a director's guidance; preachers do the work of the dramaturg and the director and the designer and the actor. We enflesh the words even as we breathe life into the characters and the text. The congregation, too, is never passive; it participates actively as part of the cast and the play. And when we preachers are lucky enough to find a truthful moment to play with our congregations, God's grace becomes as potent and relevant as any cataclysmic event. It shakes our foundations until we decide we need to take another look at where we are and where we are going.

What led me to the ministry? It wasn't the original plan. But I have faith that a circuitous route filled with curve balls and unmarked road signs can be as clear and true as morning light. I have faith that it is God who passes out the maps to a journey we wouldn't want to miss.

The Rev. Anna Carter Florence
Westminster Presbyterian Church, Minneapolis
July 15, 1990
Exodus 1:8-2:10, Romans 8:22-25

At the River's Edge

You can tell a lot about a society by looking at its children. Take the United States, for example. These days, we have daycare, Sesame Street, Nintendo, and Bart Simpson. We also have crack, street gangs, homeless children, and babies with AIDS. One out of four children in our country lives below the poverty line, and for African American families, that number increases to one out of two. In 1989, 53% of our tax dollars went to military defense instead of to education for our children. That tells you a lot about us, doesn't it?

Children are more than wet cement; they are spokespeople for our values, our choices, our circumstances, and our lifestyles.

By all rights of the law, baby Moses should have been dead. That tells you a lot about Egypt. Moses didn't start life with many advantages. He was born in the equivalent of a Hebrew refugee camp, or the Hebrew slave quarters on an Egyptian plantation. He was a boy baby, and the pharaoh, sounding a lot like King Herod in Jerusalem two thousand years later, had ordered that all male infants were to be thrown into the Nile river to drown. That tells you a lot about the Pharaoh. He'd even gone so far as to instruct the midwives and anyone else who might happen upon a woman in labor to kill the boy babies as soon as they appeared. If things had gone as the pharaoh had ordered, that ought to have taken care of Moses.

But in baby Moses' case, there were three other people the pharaoh didn't count on: the midwife, the mother of Moses, and the daughter of Pharaoh. They wouldn't play

31

ball. The midwife feared God, the mother loved her baby, and the Pharaoh's own daughter had compassion on the abandoned child. They each had to break the law to save the life of that baby. That tells you a lot about them. And they weren't saints. They were ordinary people acting under extraordinary circumstances, whose faith, love, and compassion made them more than they were.

There are theologians who will argue that this story is just a legend about a national hero, just a parallel version of a tale that exists in many other cultures. There are other theologians who insist that it was the providence of God, not a handful of scared human beings, that saved baby Moses from the fate of a thousand other Hebrew boy babies. But what interests me about this passage is the action of the story itself, the characters who labor between right and wrong at the river's edge. That's what interests me, because I know that I've been down at the river's edge almost every day of my life, sitting on the bank, watching stuff pass: the boats, the dead logs, and sometimes the babies in a basket. You can learn a lot about a culture by watching what floats by on a river, because some of it belongs there and some of it doesn't. This is a story about our ability as human beings to know the difference between those two things, or between what is kind and just and merciful, and what is cruel and unjust and abominable in the eyes of God. It's a story about breaking down stereotypes, and we can learn a lot from it.

When I was in New York last month, I went to see the new production of "The Grapes of Wrath", John Steinbeck's classic novel of the Great Depression. It's a story about an Oklahoma sharecropper family, driven off their land by big agricultural interests and, like thousands of other desperate families, lured to the promised land of California in hope of finding work. Of course there isn't anything there but dirt poor wages and strikes and corruption and starvation. They lose everything except their dignity and the will to survive.

In one of the last scenes of the play - and the novel, too - the daughter, who has been pregnant throughout the story, goes into labor in the middle of a flood and delivers a still-born baby. Her uncle John is sent out to somehow bury the baby in spite of the rising waters of the river. Listen to what Steinbeck writes:

> Uncle John...put his shovel down, and holding the box in front of him, he edged through the brush until he came to the edge of the swift stream....He held the apple box against his chest. And then he leaned over and set the box in the stream and steadied it with his hand. He said fiercely, 'Go down an' tell 'em. Go down in the street, an' rot an' tell 'em that way. That's the way you can talk. Don' even know if you was a boy or a girl. Ain't gonna find out. Go on down now, an' lay in the street. Maybe they'll know then.

You can learn a lot about the Great Depression from that scene. I know we all have stories about that period; my own family lost everything and went to California on a hoax, too. Migrant workers, farmers, factory workers and so many others suffered without a voice then, and no one seemed to hear.

Steinbeck's grim scene makes a strong statement: What does it take for us to realize that things are skewed and wrong? What does it take for us to realize that we can do better, we can BE better? If a starving migrant worker doesn't spark compassion in us, then will a baby in a box, or a basket, floating down the river? If a statistic won't do it, a statistic that tells us that one out of every two black children we meet in this country doesn't get enough to eat, then what will? We need to know what our breaking point is, don't we? - especially when we're at the river's edge. What does it take?

The pharaoh's daughter came down to the river with her entourage of servants for a swim. Who knows what she'd been brought up to believe about the Hebrews, those coarse foreigners who multiplied like rabbits in their filthy ghettoes? Presumably, she'd seem them working at a distance on yet another enormous building project. But it's hard to imagine that she'd ever actually had a conversation with a Hebrew girl her age, or broken bread with a Hebrew family.

So here she is, the princess of Egypt, taking her daily dip at the river's edge, when she sees a basket floating in the reeds, and hears something that sounds like a faint cry. One of her maids goes to fetch it, and what should be inside but a real, live baby, a squalling, hungry, frightened infant. Her first thought must have been, whose baby is this? And then: why would any mother put her baby in the river in such a carefully constructed little ark if she wasn't desperate for it to live? She looks to see if it's a boy of a girl; it's a boy, all right. And then it dawns on her: "This must be one of the Hebrew's children," she says.

Her mind must have been racing. "One of *them*," she thinks. "An actual Hebrew baby, who's going to grow up to be huge and ugly and a threat to my life, according to my father! What am I going to do? I'm supposed to kill it; I can't do that. What if I just leave it here? But then it will die anyway; how long can a baby go without milk?" And before she can decide what to do, a young girl comes bounding out of the bullrushes, saying, "Shall I go and get you a nurse from the Hebrew women to nurse that baby for you?" Obviously this is more than a coincidence; the girl means the baby's mother; she's probably his sister. And she's talking as if the baby now belonged to the Pharaoh's daughter, as if the princess, not the mother or the sister were responsible for it! The girl is talking as if they have a connection beyond the fact that they all just happen to be there together down at the river's edge: the baby, his sister, the princess and her maids. And everyone is waiting for the princess to make a decision, everyone, that is, but the baby, who just wants to be held, and fed, and given a warm place to sleep.

We know how the story ends. The princess has compassion on the baby, and probably on his family, too, and decides to save the child. She tells them that she will pay them to take care of him, and when he is older, that they should bring him back to the palace so that she can raise him as her own son. It's a huge risk for her to take, to disobey her father's law, but I think what happened is this: when she actually saw this Hebrew baby at the river's edge, and stepped into the shoes of that mother, all the things she'd been taught to believe since childhood, and all her fear and ignorance about this other group of people, just evaporated. She had a connection with someone, a relationship. No law was more important than that.

What does it take for us to realize that things have to change? What does it take for us to meet our prejudices head on? It takes a connection, a relationship. Sometimes I think it takes a baby in a basket floating at the river's edge. But it also takes an awareness that we're laboring at something that isn't finished yet. Learning to be truly open to people who are different than we are takes time, and unlearning our prejudices and fears can be painful. But when we stand at the river's edge, God gives us the strength to do what we have to do. God gives us the gifts of compassion and love to overcome our fears and pull that baby out of the water.

There is a scene from the film *Gandhi* that I will never forget. India is groaning in its labor pains to be an independent nation, and once again, it is the tragic conflict between Hindus and Muslims that is tearing things apart. The slaughter goes against everything that Gandhi, their beloved leader and the promoter of nonviolence, has worked for. And so, despite the great risks to his health, he goes on another hunger strike, vowing not to eat until the violence between Hindus and Muslims ceases. Many days go by; the fighting rages on, and Gandhi's physicians tell him that given his frail state of health, if he does not eat soon, he will die. One morning, a ragged Muslim man makes his way into Gandhi's bedroom, hurls a piece of bread at him, and says, "Here, eat this! I'm already going to hell, but I don't want your death on my conscience too!" Gandhi asks him quietly, "What do you want?" And the man says, "Last night, my only son was killed in the riots by a Hindu. And I was so full of grief and rage that I went out and took a baby Hindu boy, and I smashed him against a wall until his head broke open. I know I'm going to hell. But you mustn't die for us, or we will have twice the torment." Gandhi thinks a moment, and then asks him, "You are a Muslim?" "Yes," the man says, "I am." "Then what you must do," Gandhi tells him, "is to go out and find a Hindu boy whose father was killed last night. Take him home and adopt him to be your only son, and raise him to be a good Hindu."

The Hebrew people couldn't soften the hearts of the Pharaoh and his daughter. But a mother who couldn't keep her own baby put him in a basket at the river's edge, hoping that someone would see him and have pity on him. And someone did. The pharaoh's own daughter came down to the banks of the Nile and got her first real look at a Hebrew family, her first real taste of the miserable dilemma they were in, and she did what she could. She said, enough. Enough fear. Enough hatred. Enough ignorance. This baby is laboring to be somebody, and I've got to labor at it, too. I've got to realize that the water has broken, and nothing can hold this baby back from coming; not the law, not the Pharaoh, nothing. I've got a connection with this baby because we're both here at the river's edge, and I can do something to help it. And then I'll never be able to look at another Hebrew without seeing my own son.

What are we laboring for down at the river's edge? What old fears and stereotypes and worn out ways are we clinging to down in the bullrushes? Well, stand guard, because God is breaking the waters around us, the labor pains are fierce, and the baby in the basket is on its way. Nothing we can do to stop the pain, nothing we can do to push the baby back. We've got to reach in there and pick it up and say,

> *"Yes, you're my son. You're my daughter.*
> *Doesn't matter what color you are; you're my sister.*
> *Doesn't matter what religion you are; you're my*
> *brother. I don't care what I used to believe, you can*
> *love anyone you want to, male or female. You don't*
> *have to grow up to be smart, or pretty, or strong, or*
> *perfect, because I don't care. It's all right. Don't you*
> *cry any-more. We'll just sit here together, down*
> *at the river's edge. We'll just sit here."*

Drawing by Susan Friesen

The Rev. Anna Carter Florence
Westminster Presbyterian,Minneapolis
December 30, 1990
Luke 2:21-40; Matthew 2:13-33

A Blessing and a Sword

By the Sunday after Christmas, we've had our shepherds and angels and wise men and babies. We're knee-deep in gift exchanges, steeped in togetherness, and the familiar carols may have started sounding like a broken record. We're ready for what Frederick Buechner writes about Christmas in his book, _Whistling in the Dark_:

> _The Word become flesh. Ultimate Mystery born with a skull you could crush one handed. Incarnation._
> _It is not tame. It is not touching. It is not beautiful. It is uninhabitable terror. It is unthinkable darkness, riven with unbearable light.... You can only cover your eyes and shudder before it._

That's a long way from "Silent Night" and "The First Noel." Buechner's point is that when we peel back the well-intentioned layers of choreography, Christmas is more Martha Graham than Shirley Temple. We spend four weeks preparing to receive a baby into our lives, four weeks doing our best to be merry and musical and focused and extravagant within our means, and it is good and right that we should be moved on Christmas Eve, moved to tears and song. But the real miracle has to do with the wildness and strangeness of God's grace. As Buechner says, God-with-us is not tame. It is not touching or beautiful. It is uninhabitable terror, unthinkable darkness riven with unthinkable light.

This may not be as evident on Christmas Eve, when the shepherds are gathered round and angels are singing and the Little Lord Jesus is asleep on the hay. It is very much in evidence only a few days later.

The instant we leave the Hallmark creche with the Madonna in blue, we are plunged into a world that is not the way we like to remember Bethlehem, yet is the real Bethlehem. The moment we turn our ears from the heavenly host singing, "Glory to God in the highest, and on earth peace, goodwill to all," we hear prophecies that make parents weep, that chill them to their very bones.

I'm not trying to ruin a beautiful week by regaling you with horror stories from Scripture. These events aren't in the Bible to scare us, or to knock our sugar-plumed heads back into reality before the new year begins and things get back to normal. What happens in Bethlehem and Jerusalem in the first few days after Jesus' birth doesn't change the fact that unto us is born in the city of David a savior, who is Christ the Lord. What does change is how we live with this news, how we make sense of it, how we are transformed by it.

Imagine for a moment that we have only a few frames of a long film. Matthew and Luke are like masterful camera men; zoom in with them for a close-up of the sweetness of the stable, pan out, and suddenly the whole content of the scene comes into focus, and you realize that the mass of darkness you thought was just the night sky is really a panorama of hills, and houses, and people running in the night. That's what the days after Christmas are like: focusing on all the blurry material in the background. And what do we see?

Matthew and Luke are clearly filming on two sides of town. Neither one of them seems to have a clue about what the other is doing. Matthew and Luke are not collaborators. These are two distinct perspectives, complete with different casts and different scripts, of how Jesus and his family spent the first few days after his birth.

In Luke's drama, the first thing we see is that the best

lines don't go to Mary or Joseph, and that the center of the scene isn't even Jesus; it's Simeon and Anna who steal the show. Simeon and Anna were two pious old prophets who had earned sainthood not by their deeds, but by their patience. They were waiting to see the Messiah before they died. Who knows if they were expecting him to come riding in on a horse with flaming swords, or descending from the sky with armies of angels? They may not have known themselves.

But on this particular day, the Messiah arrives at the temple in diapers, and one look is all it takes for them to recognize him. Simeon takes the baby in his arms and blesses him with a full, rich blessing about what a light he will be to the world. And then, as he hands the baby back to his parents, he looks in their eyes and adds a troubling footnote: "This child is destined for the falling and the rising of many in Israel," he says, "and to be a sign that will be opposed so that the inner thoughts of many will be revealed - and a sword will pierce your own soul too." That's the first scene. It's a blessing with a double-edged sword.

Matthew, on the other hand, has an completely different idea of the post-Christmas scene. His version is more graphic; there are strange dreams, and dramatic escapes, and violence. King Herod couldn't stand the thought that the wise men had duped him, but even worse than that was the thought that for all his tremendous power, somewhere in the Bethlehem area was an infant who was more powerful than he.

And so he did what the foolish and powerful do when they panic: he blamed the most vulnerable and innocent, and he made them pay. He ordered all children under the age of two to be killed - not just boy babies, as tradition has told us, but girls too, in a vicious and extravagant act of vengeance. Of course, Jesus escaped; Joseph was warned in a dream, and in an extraordinary shift from Old

Testament themes, spirited the family *into* Egypt rather than out of it, because now the enemy was at home in Israel. But the children of Bethlehem, scores of them, did not escape; their parents had no dreams, and they perished, every one of them. That's what Matthew's camera sees. That's what's going on in the blurry darkness behind the stable.

Two film clips, then. A blessing and a sword. A prophecy and a nightmare.

The week after Christmas, and this is what we see simultaneously on two different screens. It would be a lot easier if we could focus on only one of them, choose the blessing, for instance, and ignore the sword. But we can't do that; we can't isolate single frames once we've seen the whole picture. That's what the world does to us; that's what it is; dozens of film projectors running at once in a darkened room, where we have to sit and watch.

Christ our Savior is born, we sang, just days ago; sleep in heavenly peace. Outside, the streets are filled with terror, and the fact remains that while the Messiah has come, we are slammed into the harsh reality that at this stage, it may not make any difference. The children are being slaughtered around us; the souls of countless parents are pierced through. Yesterday was the 100th anniversary of the massacre at Wounded Knee, South Dakota, in which 300 Lakota Indians, most of them women and children, were slaughtered by U.S. troops. There has hardly been a word about it in the press. Wounded Knee might as well be Bethlehem - it *is* Bethlehem. What can a baby do to stop that? What can a baby do to counter a Herod, except escape in the night?

The harsh reality is that we have to wait. The world had to wait thirty years for this child to grow up; we have to wait for God's time, despite the fact that we need that baby *now*. My God, we need him now. But coming in the form of human flesh means that God, like all of us, has to be nurtured by human parents and allowed to grow and develop in human years; the baby is not automatically a king. He has to grow to be a king. And he can't do it alone; he has to be nursed and held and comforted and disciplined and taught and loved and befriended and challenged. And the awesome question is what part we play in that. Does it matter if we nurture the Christ, or not? Does it matter whether we abuse power or not? Of course it does. In the end, it matters not so much to the child and his family, who seem to have special dispensation from the angels, but it matters deeply to us. It matters to the children of Bethlehem and their parents. It matters to everyone in the blurry background, and we are all there.

The point is that the child will grow up to be a king, helped along by the human family. The Christ will grow in each of us. But meanwhile, we have to fulfill our part of the prophecy in order to make it so. We have to decide between blessings and swords, when it is ours to decide, and we have to deal with the blessings and the swords when they come to us without our doing.

And so now it is New Year's Eve, and I wonder how you are. I wonder what you hope or fear for yourself and your family this coming year. I wish I could say that 1991 only holds God's richest blessings for us all, and in the deepest sense I believe that this is so, but in the day to day world of human times, we know that there will be swords for us as well. Each of us is poised on the brink of a new year with a baby in our arms, and it's hard to know whether we're running away in the dark, or receiving a blessing in the temple. Where are we in the picture? What will happen to us?

Our lives read like a gospel. Some are like Matthew, some like Luke. Some of us this year will know mostly swords, some of us will receive blessings, and there is no reason or fairness for any of it. But the screens run side by side; we can look around to see what's playing right next to us. The characters and plots may differ from scene to scene; if we look closely, the Christ child is in every one of them.

The light of the world has come into all our lives; we are all the living gospel, the good news, the divine cinema. People look at us and can read what God has written and directed there, and how we have chosen to play the scene without any rehearsals, and more than not, God-with-us is not tame, or beautiful. Sometimes it is Buechner's uninhabitable terror, unthinkable darkness, and we just want to cover our eyes at what we see playing on the screen, what we're asked to do and bear. That's the sword that pierces our hearts.

But the sword cannot be the last scene. It isn't the last scene. Somewhere in the fullness of time, that baby has grown up and become a man, an extraordinary man, who has more than a few scenes to play with you. These scenes will not all be about Herod, and running away in the dark. There will be blessings. Because the baby survived, there will be blessings for you, too. And there will be peace on earth, heavenly peace, because that is what we were promised just a few nights ago, and the promise is real. It is real.

You do not go alone into the night of the new year. You go with scripts for a blessing and a sword in your hand, and a mandate to play them both, the best that you know how. You go with God's wild and strange grace to guide you. You go with the baby in your arms, and Christ at your side.   Go   in   peace.

Reverend M. Susan Milnor

The Rev. M. Susan Milnor

Born: Knoxville, Tennessee
Religious Background: Unitarian Universalist; raised Southern Baptist
Education: B.A. With Highest Honors, M.A. in English Literature, Univ. of Tennessee; M. Div., Harvard Divinity School
Employment: co-minister, First Universalist Church, Minneapolis (preaching and worship duties; pastoral care; adult education; administration); formerly minister at Unitarian Universalist Fellowship of Macon, Georgia; Instructor of English, Auburn Univ. and Piedmont Virginia Community College, Charlottesville, Virginia.
Personal: Married to Terry Sweetser (co-minister at First Universalist); daughter Abigail, one year
Interests and Hobbies: movies from the Thirties and Forties; walking; writing poetry; Southern literature; passions are the coast of Maine, the Appalachian mountains; strong commitments to women's rights, environmental issues (especially coastal concerns); civil rights. And my daughter!

Ministry is for me, above all, about relatedness. The heart of my ministry is my relationship to the members of the congregation I serve, as well as to the larger community.

Indeed, it was because of the relationships I had been blessed with in my life that I entered the ministry. The love I had received and been invited to give, the experiences I had shared with people, the friendships that had made the world hospitable to me - all these seemed, by my mid-thirties, to be precious gifts. Somehow, I wanted to "give back" something to other people. At the same time I had begun to feel "called" to the ministry. This sense of calling became a conviction that all the paths of my living had converged, almost inescapably, into the journey of ordained ministry. It was as if ministry chose me, rather than that I chose it. What I felt called to do, above all, was to strive to speak the truth in love, serve with respect for others and for self, and to be faithful to God.

Not surprisingly, relatedness is also central to the theology that informs and, I hope, "enspirits" my ministry. The divine is most often manifest, it seems to me, in the transforming love that bonds people to one another in relationship and in community. Furthermore, that love has the most saving potential of almost anything we experience in our living. My preaching, as well as my own spirituality, depends heavily on an awareness of the patterns of meaning and hope that emerge from the web of relations in which we live. I call the visibility of those patterns to us grace.

Since I serve a congregation with several hundred members, Sunday morning worship is the context of my relatedness to many people. That makes preaching especially important to me. Ideally, a sermon invites people to call on their own experience and wisdom, their memories, their joy and their pain, in order to find renewal or grow toward greater wholeness.

I continue to be struck by the fact that I don't know the power of a sermon until I preach it - until people in the congregation receive and interact with it. Whatever life a sermon has, it takes on in the presence and attention of others. On paper a sermon consists of ideas, confessions, stories. Delivered in community, those same elements together, at their best, become witness. Perhaps that is the working of the Spirit.

The rewards of preaching are many, for example helping to create moments of sacred time, and being of help to people in finding the shape of their journeys. As an extrovert, I love to deliver sermons. The frustrations are real, too. Sometimes, the writing is agonizing - truly a kind of giving birth. Trying to touch something deep for people makes preaching a considerable responsibility.

Many of the other rewards of ministry also grow out of the relationships. I feel especially privileged to be present in people's lives during the "deep moments" - times of joy, times of grief, times of passage and transformation. These moments come in rites, such as child dedications, weddings and memorial services; in counseling; in simple befriending. The privilege is first simply to know others. Secondly, it is to experience sacred moments of life, which, because of their sanctity, become eternal. At such times I feel the divine presence in the delicate strands holding us all together in the web of creation. I feel as if I have died, and am being born, as I look into the past and into the future.

Ironically, many of the frustrations of ministry are also effects of relatedness. I use so much of my energy for people in my work that I am not able to nurture friendships as well as I used to. Also, the constant emotional complexity of interacting with so many people can be tiring.

The longer I am in ministry, the more aware I am of the challenges for a woman in this life. Sometimes they are external, for example when the parents of two persons whose wedding I am conducting are upset that the minister is a woman. The greater challenges are internal, though. As someone whose job it is to serve others, I struggle not to feel caught in the traditional female role of responding to others and neglecting myself.

The joys of being a woman in ministry are significant as well. These include bringing a woman's voice to the pulpit, a woman's presence to religious leadership, a woman's concerns and conscience to decision making. Other women's need for that presence makes it a special joy. And what a mutual ministry it is! The women in my church are wonderful; constantly they teach, inspire and empower me, making it possible for me to minister to all of the people in our community.

Thirteen women in my congregation made a beautiful patchwork quilt for my infant daughter. On one of the squares they embroidered the words with which my co-minister husband and I often close our prayers: "May our hopes and dreams take flight on the wings of love."

Surely, my ministry is kept aloft by the love in our community.

The Rev. M. Susan Milnor
First Universalist Church, Minneapolis
May 13, 1990

Sarah Laughed

*(Dedicated to my husband and to my daughter
Abigail's primary care nurses at Minneapolis Children's
Hospital's Newborn Intensive Care Unit: Angi, Debi,
Jeannine, and Lynn.)*

You may recall the tale of Sarah in the Book of Genesis.
Sarah is ninety years old and her husband Abraham older
when God announces that Sarah will bear a child. Sarah
responds by laughing.

Deeply offended, God asks why she's laughing, making
the point, I suppose, that he can do anything. It would
thus seem that one of the real themes of the story is faith
(and also honesty, because Sarah tries to deny that she
laughed.)

What interests me, though, is Sarah's laughter. There's
something very human in her inability to believe she will
become a mother. It's too incredible. Not natural. Not the
way things are supposed to be.

This story is relevant today, on Mother's Day, because
many of us are unaware of the mothering in our lives when
it happens - both the mothering we do and the mothering
we receive. We are so unaware of it, in fact, that we would
laugh if someone called it that. We would not believe it.

For the past two years I have spoken about Mother's
Day from the pulpit of this church. In both cases, I have
told stories about birth mothers and grandmothers, family
legacies passed on. For many people, most of us perhaps,
the topics carry a special power. After all, at the very least,
each of us had a birth mother.

At the same time, doing so makes me a little uneasy.

The difficulty in both having and being mothers has left many people with pain. There are people here who would like to have children by birth and cannot. There are people here who have lost children, and who have lost dreams about children. There are same sex couples here for whom the reality of parenting is even more complex than it is for most people. There are parents here who have adopted children and whom the language of Mother's Day sometimes excludes.

These people are not laughing. It is their exclusion, their loneliness, their grief that bothers me. It especially bothers me when I look at the greeting cards, the advertisements, the images of Mother's Day. It would seem that mothering always take place in a white, middle class American family comprised of one man, one woman and probably two children, both born easily and healthily.

The point is not to make middle class families with birth children feel guilty. Indeed, you - we - should enjoy the day and celebrate. The point is this: the superficial images alone do not help us really to appreciate mothering, to see its depths and its mystery, its truly sacred aspect.

The greetings cards would have us believe that mothering depends solely on what you are. But mothering is also a matter of what you do, and it's at the juncture of the two - when what you do determines what you are - that mystery is tapped and the holy is found. That mystery is what I would invite us, as a religious community, to celebrate.

The good news is this, the great opportunity of it is that mothering can be given or received by anyone. Each of us, at some point, is Sarah laughing.

If there is anyone who does not expect to be a mother, anyone who might be Sarah, it is men. During my pregnancy Terry often thought and talked of fathering, but if a voice from the heavens had spoken to him of mothering, he would have laughed. Indeed, it became a joke between us, when I would say that I was carrying this child for nine months and once she was born, it would be his turn for the next nine. (As it turns out, I guess he owes me only six.)

Life works out strangely, though. There is much I will never forget about the first days of my daughter Abigail's life, but one of the most poignant was my husband's presence by her side. From the beginning, he was there for her and has never let up. And in the trauma, the fear, the uncertainty of those first days, he was her mainstay. He visited her at least twice every day. He sat by her isolette, talking to her sometimes for forty-five minutes at a stretch, urging her to live, telling her of his faith that she would do so. He put his hands on her tiny, fragile body and held her still in her agitation. He sat beside her and loved her. He murmured over her and called relatives to tell them about her. He did all those things a mother is "supposed" to do.

All this when her biological mother was first too sick, then too distraught, too filled with fear and pain to do the mothering. I was her mother, but it was her father who mothered her. Over and over, I thought how lucky she was, no, how blessed, to have a father who could mother her.

It raises the question of what we mean by mothering. Mothering is supposed to be the soft love, the nourishing of a human being and a human spirit. Feeding and touching and reassuring. In contrast, the stereotype of fathering in our culture is of a tougher love. It has something to do with being there, at least at times, and with providing and guiding and disciplining. Something to do with crises and milestones.

The reality, though, is that increasingly those distinctions - to the extend they were ever true - are breaking down. More often parents of either sex perform both roles and the goal is more holistic parenting. Perhaps that's what makes the celebration of Mother's Day - or

Father's Day - a little more cloudy than it used to be. In some ways, it is as if we should, on both occasions, celebrate Parents' Day.

But Mother's Day it is, and so today we celebrate that nourishing quality, that soft love. And one of the values in my recent experience for me has been learning to appreciate the many, many kinds of mothering that fall outside the Hallmark greeting boundaries. Yes, I know from experience the special bonds that bearing a child create; they are real. But there are many other special bonds as well.

The bond between a father and a child he mothers is special and equally precious in its own way. The bonds adoptive parents make with their children are special and equally precious. No, they did not choose to bring these human beings into the world, but they chose to bring them into their lives. What a risk, what confidence in life and love that takes. What mothering and fathering and parenting.

Within the ranks of adoptive parents are those who take into their lives children of another culture. The confusing, often lonely process of doing this, the prejudices the whole family faces here, the challenges of understanding and communication - all these require special mothering. And they create special bonds.

Foster parents, too, give great gifts and make special ties. To risk attachment, to risk pain, to risk the disillusionment and disappointment of seeing a child put on a path you would not choose for him or her takes courage. What mothering. What nurturing of human life and spirit because it is right and good and necessary, because the very divinity in every human being calls us to do it.

Same sex couples, too, face special pain and challenges. One of the challenges is that we break this sacred, mysterious act of caring for a young life into mothering and fathering. How difficult for families, friends, even couples themselves to sort this out.

But the truth is perhaps more simple than our ideas of it. Mothering is part of parenting, part of the whole. And it is also a very human act that we can give to and receive from friends, mentors, all kinds of people in our lives. Its ultimate importance lies in the value it places on human life.

This brings me to the final category of people whose mothering, whose parenting, I want to celebrate. It is those people who care for others in the course of a job but who bring a special, sacred gift of love and nurturing to it. People who do this transcend a job and touch the mystery of life itself.

Consider child care providers. Surely, we are so aware of abuse in this area that we sometimes forget the acts of love and guidance and caring - the mothering - that devoted childcare givers pour out every day.

But the place I have seen and felt this most graphically is among the primary care nurses at the Newborn Intensive Care Unit of Children's Hospital. There are over 100 nurses on this unit, and in order to provide continuity of care to particular babies, they have what is called a primary nurse care system. Individual nurses can sign up to be "primaries" for particular babies. That means that whenever possible they are assigned to care for that baby and that they have a special responsibility for her care.

The nurses on this unit are highly competent professionals. In moments of crisis or question, they click into clinical performance. They are knowledgeable and can be detached in their assessment of situations. Primaries turn their professional competence into art by knowing a particular baby well - her needs, reactions, etc., and adjusting medical care accordingly.

But the primaries do so much more. They become attached to the infant and sometimes come to love her.

They get to know the parent or parents and form relationships with them. They help parents accept the bizarre and abnormal circumstances of their children's entry into life. And in the process, they do a lot of mothering. Mothering of both babies and parents. Mothering that might follow Sarah's laughter.

I remember the first time I came in to find Abigail dressed in clothes - a long white gown with pink flowers. Her primary nurse who did this had mentioned for days that soon we could dress her. She probably saw the parents - or at least the mother - shrink from this idea. Treating a tiny creature as a normal baby in the strange world of intensive care is difficult.

But I saw her dressed and a whisper in my heart said, "That's my little girl." And a few days later I realized something else. While I had not wanted to look at the first pictures of Abigail, red and scrawny and naked, I could look at the ones in which she was dressed. Then I developed an interest in the premature baby clothes sold from glass cases at the unit. Previously, I had walked by, avoiding looking at them. Now I began to stop and window shop. As her primary nurses themselves got Abigail a few things (believing, perhaps, that her parents were going to leave her naked forever), I finally took courage in hand and joyfully purchased my first items.

Dressing a baby. Such a small thing, an act of mothering. And in this case, the nurse mothered me as well, mothered me into being a parent. Sarah laughed.

So many things have been like that. Her primaries kept asking if I wanted to hold her inside the isolette when she had to be lifted up, say for a bedding change. I shrank and said no. I was afraid of hurting her, afraid of feeling and not just seeing how small she was. Finally, one night, after her dad had courageously complied, and her mom declined, one of her primaries gently insisted. I stuck my hands into the isolette, and she gently laid this tiny creature into them. I wept for it being so right. And because of her nurse, I was a little closer not to just *being* Abigail's mother, but much more importantly, to mothering Abigail. Sarah laughed.

There are many other stories. The primary who got Abigail a pink Easter dress and taught us that a holiday could include our baby, too. And who made her a big beautiful birthday card with clowns to mark her one month birthday.

Or the primary who made another card for Abigail reading: "I'm Abigail. Watch me grow." Every week on Thursday, her birth day, this nurse has hung a number carefully cut from construction paper marking the week and recording her weight. The rising numbers have helped us believe our baby will come home.

Now these women - sorry, but all the nurses on the unit are women - are careful not to try to *be* the baby's mother. They are meticulous about encouraging the parents to bond with the child, to take part in the physical care of the child when she is stable enough. They are insistent, and persistent, in telling the parents how important our being there is to the baby. They assure parents the babies recognize our voices and smells.

But let's be clear. In reality, these primary nurses do most of the acts of mothering in the first weeks of life of these premature babies. They change diapers, clean the babies, touch them, pat them, talk to them. And they do the most important thing mothers are supposed to do: that is, treat this new life as a human being, to be nourished and loved, appreciated and respected. Most importantly, they do this when biological parents may be having more than a little trouble functioning.

Like her father, these women, too, have mothered my baby. They have nourished her spirit and soul as well as her body. They have helped her live, not just with superb medical care, but with love.

She is lucky to have had so many mothers. And to her primary nurses I say this: You have never threatened the fact that I am her mother; you have helped me know it and love it. You have never made me jealous; you have given me confidence. You have never lost my respect as professionals; you have magnified it. You have mothered my baby and I will be grateful to you for as long as I live. And in those acts of mothering, you have, for mysterious moments, become a mother to her. And a mother to me. The doing leads to the being. You are Sarah. We are all laughing. Happy Mother's Day.

And to all the people here who are not mothers solely by virtue of giving birth, but rather by virtue of nourishing a human life, a soul, a psyche, Sarah laughs for you. To every person in this room who has mothered someone in a moment of need and restored some faith in life, Sarah laughs for you. To adoptive parents, whose choice is as precious as any, Sarah laughs for you. To all the people who have found a way to be whole parents, for moments or weeks, or months, Sarah laughs for you.

To all the fathers who open themselves to the nourishing parent within, on this Mother's Day, Sarah laughs for you. To all who nourish another human life through touch and care and love, Sarah laughs for you. What you do is a sacred act of life, an act that makes life holy. Sarah laughs today. It echoes in our ears.

Drawing by Susan Friesen

The Rev. M. Susan Milnor
First Universalist Church, Minneapolis
April 21, 1991

In Touch with the Wind

The path ahead, it seems, stretches eternally to nowhere, but because eternally, to everywhere. Underfoot, inches of brown needles strew softness onto the ground. Overhead, trees intertwine against the sky to form contrasts so stark they catch even a young infant's eyes each time she passes.

To one side, the path tumbles down rocks into a cove. Rising and falling, the tide tells its ancient story in the lapping of water. To the other side of the path, woods hold the unseen. Perhaps a snake will cross, or a fox or deer stand in silent alert.

All is not beauty. Sometimes there is death on the path. Sometimes a cry - was it the thrilled shriek of an osprey rising from the water, silver fish glinting in talons? Or was it - you might just imagine - the fish's scream of agony as its world disappears?

Yes, the path goes somewhere. It comes to a halt. A point of rock. The land's end. And the world has opened; the horizon is everywhere and everything. It is the sea.

Land's end - no other place on earth so powerful for me. Yet, the path draws me back. To walk slowly, to stop, to sit. To feel the wind touch my face, to sense it move through me to the universe. To just be there, so that there I can just be.

And there, if it will ever happen, I will fall in love again, with this home, the world. And there on the path, if anywhere, I will know life in its original blessing.

This path is a place I love, in Maine. And this meditation about it is uttered from my sense of the First Path of Creation Spirituality. This is the "via positiva" -

the path of awe. The commandment for being on this path is "Thou shalt fall in love three times daily."

What a strange religious commandment. But an appropriate one to explore this Earth Day morning. And on this day, when we would honor the earth, when we would dedicate ourselves to her survival, we are called to be not just ecologists, but lovers of creation as well. We are called to fall in love with the universe and to spread our love until once again we stand in sacred relation to what it is.

Creation Spirituality is both a tradition and a movement. It is a tradition of many native peoples, in Eastern religions, and it is even a tradition within Christianity. There, it is found more clearly in a line of medieval mystic prophets such as Hildegarde of Bingen, Meister Eckhart, Julian of Norwich, Francis of Assissi. These mystics are remarkable for the gracefulness of creation in their vision, for the sensuousness of their praise, for their affirmation of spirit and matter as one.

Creation spirituality is not only a tradition, however; it is also a movement: alive, breathing, changing, reaching toward the future. Its adherents are determined not by labels or denominations, but rather by a stance toward the universe.

From this point of view, the creation is sacred, all-holy, to be revered, and it is holy because it is. Centuries ago Meister Eckhart said, "*isness* is God." And he speaks to us still. Molecules, atoms, stars, galaxies, creatures, people - all are; all are good; are all divine.

Perhaps in your head you say that's obvious. But in our hearts it is not. We come from a long religious and cultural heritage, the dominant voice of which says there is something wrong with the creation; it's in a sinful state; it is less than god, less than good. This heritage assumes that creation is stagnant, its myth that the world was created in six days, and then creation is at an end. Those who practice Creation Spirituality, however, see creation as the once begun, ongoing, constantly changing process of life.

All of these ideas are good ones, vitally important to us on Earth Day. But I believe that without a religiously deep revolution in our feeling for the creation, our efforts to treat our planet more justly, more compassionately, perhaps to save it, will not be enough. People are not motivated by guilt; we are motivated by love and reverence.

But neither are ideas enough. We talked about creation, but the other part of all this is spirituality. The word "spirit" is derived from the Hebrew root,"ruah," meaning breath, or wind. To be spiritual means to be fully alive, filled with the breath of life, "in touch with the wind," as Matthew Fox says. It means to follow a life-filled path, a spirit-filled way of living. It usually involves a discipline, a path, the point of which is not the end, but a way of being on it. To live the creation; to breath it; to be touched by its winds. That's what we are talking about.

Rabbi Abraham Heschel writes that there are three responses possible to the creation: "We may exploit it; we may enjoy it; we may accept it with awe." Surely on this Earth Day, we are aware of how the Earth is exploited, and we know that is not the right way. Perhaps, though, it's only somewhat better to enjoy the creation. For to enjoy still means a mentality of consuming and using. The earth, the creation, becomes a means to pleasure and entertainment. Indeed, enjoyment implies a distanced relationship. To accept with awe is the way of Creation Spirituality. Thus comes the injunction to fall in love daily.

John Dobson is a person who does this and even manages to share his reverence with other people. Dobson is what he calls a sidewalk astronomer. One night he had a chance to look through a telescope at the moon. He was filled with awe. "My God," he thought, "everybody's got to see this." Long a man of mission, he began to share the moon with others.

Now he drives a brightly-colored van painted on the side with large letters "Sidewalk Astronomer." In it he carries a decent little telescope. He travels around the country, stopping at national and state parks, campgrounds, anywhere he can share his passion with other human beings. When he finds a group of interested people, and a clear night, he holds a "Star Party." "The only price of admission," he says, "is curiosity." Dobson wants people to feel the awe "in their guts," and he wants, above all, for them to be aware of their relationship to this magnificent creation in which they live. When someone thanks him for showing them sun spots, he replies, "Don't thank me. It's your sun."

It's not just in the face of the heavens that we experience such mystery. It's not just on the end of a telescope that we fall in love. If we are but willing, it happens in all of our lives. It happens when we see the colors of the prairie, or climb above the clouds in the mountains. It happens when a fog descends or a tree blooms. But it also happens in our human connections. It happens whenever new life is created in birth. It happens when life is resurrected after pain, and despair takes you as low as you can go, and with someone's love you begin to rise again. It happens with the peace that can accompany death. "There is no creation/that does not have a radiance," says Hildegarde; "It could not be creation without it."

If we accept the blessing of creation, the gift of it, we are able in our time to turn that blessing outward to the world again. In that spirit, to honor this Earth Day, I offer these beatitudes:

Blessed is matter unseen, moving and being, evolving unknown, making mystery to keep souls alive, filled by the wind, calling to us.

Blessed are galaxies, gathering worlds unto worlds, whirling through time and through space, hurtling through minds, bringing us short of breath, touched by the wind, to say "Yes."

Blessed are the stars, for from them life comes, stars run their course and stars just begun, all of the stars, furnaces of life, relating all to all.

Blessed is our sun, universe brought close, warming the earth, giving us life, growing us now.

Blessed is the earth, blue-green mother of us, shedding her tears, sacred clothes rent, but blessing us still, making us hers.

Blessed are creatures of earth, sharing this home, sprung from the same atoms as we, knowing the world, not knowing it, too, part of the gift.

Blessed are we, stuff of the stars, universe made to understand, given to live and love and to die. Blessed are we, standing in awe, struggling to be whole, opening our arms, lovers of creation, in touch with the wind.

Blessed is it all, all our relations, blessed into one. Blessed is it all

Rabbi Cheryl M. Rosenstein (right)

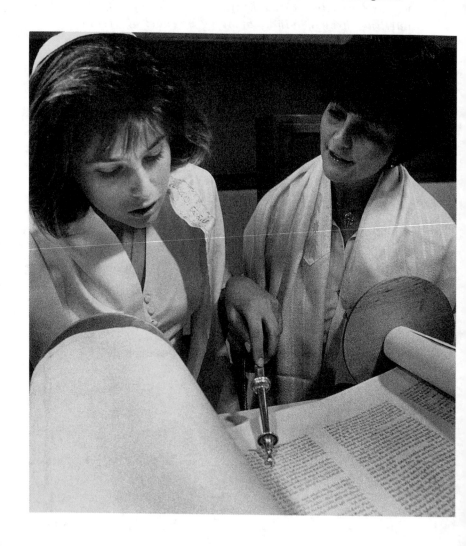

Rabbi Cheryl M. Rosenstein

Born: Long Beach, California
Religious background: Reform Jew; raised in Reform synagogue
Educational background: B.A. With Honors in Sociology, University of California, Santa Barbara; M.A.H.L. from Hebrew Union College - Jewish Institute of Religion.
Employment: Assistant Rabbi of Mt. Zion Temple, St. Paul (youth programming; "Jewish Outreach" to unaffiliated and to elderly; visiting the sick; overseeing Hebrew Department of religious school program); formerly student pulpits in Kalamazoo, Michigan; Modesto, California, and Naval Weapons Center Hebrew Congregation in China Lake, California.
Personal: married to Richard Shiell, landscape architect
Interests and hobbies: singing and Israeli folkdancing; long walks, reading. Strong commitments to issues of social justice (hunger, homelessness, the plight of the elderly), Jewish education.

As one of approximately two hundred women in the rabbinate, I am considered by some to be a pioneer. Yet I have found my road as a woman rabbi to be remarkably smooth. The real pioneers are the women who paved my way, the women who were ordained in the 1970's. They are truly a source of inspiration to me, and I owe them my deep gratitude.

I made the decision to enter the rabbinate between my sophomore and junior years of college. I was a sociology major at the University of California at Santa Barbara, trying to decide what I would do with the rest of my life. The rabbinate was not an immediately obvious choice; it was a conclusion I reached gradually and researched carefully. But upon reflection, it was a very logical choice.

My reasons for choosing the rabbinate were many and varied, altruistic and also selfish. But the most compelling

65

reason was that I would be able to live my commitment to Judaism. Had I chosen any other profession I might have had to make compromises regarding my observance of kashrut, the Sabbath and the Jewish holidays. As a rabbi, I don't need to make excuses. I can live my life honestly, with a sense of wholeness that I might otherwise not have had.

I find the rabbinate to be a totally fulfilling experience. I am never bored. I get to work with people. I teach adults as well as children. I see people through their most sacred moments: birth, coming-of-age, conversion, marriage, anniversaries, death. I continuously acquire new skills and hone my abilities through what I do, whether I'm creating liturgy and curricula, organizing programs, or dealing with people in a variety of contexts. I have opportunities to study the things I want to learn. I can even incorporate my hobbies into my work: I can sing while I pray, teach my congregants how to dance, and exercise my writing skills with every sermon and bulletin article.

I get to do all of these wonderful things in pursuit of my highest ideal: the preservation of a people, a faith and a heritage.

In rabbinical school I was taught that each of us has only one bell to ring, and that each sermon is merely a repetition or variation on that message. I try to speak on a variety of subjects. I've written "social awareness" sermons on aging and ecology, "teaching sermons" on the value of various Jewish rituals and observances, and sermons about spirituality and personal ethical behavior. But if I had to name the theme that all of them have in common, I would say that they are all about how to make Judaism more relevant for today's Jews. Because that is my mission in the rabbinate. My job is to show people the enduring value and beauty of an ancient heritage, to teach them that Judaism is still relevant to their everyday lives; that, in fact, living Jewishly can help make their lives more meaningful.

I find preaching to be a most effective means of reaching out to people. A carefully-worded message spoken from the bima (pulpit) can be a powerful tool; it can have profound effect on those who hear it. The greatest frustrations come from the writing process itself; I can always go back and improve on the sermons, polish them.

As a woman, I am part of a movement for change, not just in the rabbinate or even in the world of clergy, but for the working world in general. Traditionally, the rabbinate has been an all-consuming commitment for those who undertake it; as a profession, it encourages workaholism. While we know that we can't possibly be all things to all people, as rabbis we always *try*. The result, all too often, is that we're there for everyone - everyone but ourselves and our families.

I think that the presence of women in the rabbinate is working to restore our collective sense of balance. I believe that we are heightening the awareness that a healthy life is a balanced life - not only among our male colleagues, but among our congregants as well. Congregations are becoming more sensitive to the needs of rabbis as *human beings* - not as the "deified entities" they have often perceived us to be. Rabbinic contracts today include clauses concerning maternity and paternity leave. Rabbis are getting the message that to be a role model, they must live their lives in reality, not in the fantasies that we and our congregations create for us.

Rabbi Cheryl Rosenstein
February 8, 1991 24 Shevat, 5751
Shabbat Shekalim
Mount Zion Temple, St. Paul

It's Adar - Be Happy?

In the Hebrew month of Adar, which this year begins
next Friday, we are told to "be happy." Adar is associated
with the most joyous holiday in the Jewish calendar -
Purim. At Purim we stuff ourselves with hamentaschen,
listen to the megillah being read, and make all kinds of
racket when we hear the names of the heroes and villains of
the story. We wear colorful costumes and hold parades and
carnivals.

This is the Purim we know and love. But there are other
aspects of Purim with which we are less familiar - parts of
the story we don't pay attention to, and observances which
we've come to ignore.

Recently, some people who have read the Megillah of
Esther closely - liberal Jews, like you and me - have begun
to object to the customary merriment of Purim. They point
out that the story of Esther contains ideas that are not
consistent with modern Jewish liberal values. Esther is not
such a heroine, they say, nor is Mordecai such a hero.

To illustrate their reasons for these objections, I
thought I should tell you a story.

Once upon a time in a land called Shushan, there lived
a king whose name was Ahaseuerus. One day, Ahaseuerus
became displeased with his wife, Queen Vashti, because she
disobeyed a royal command. She had the self-respect not to
allow herself to be treated like a sex object. Because she
would not dance naked before the king and his drunken
cronies, she was dethroned and beheaded.

To replace his queen with a more beautiful and
obedient woman, the king staged a beauty pageant, in the

course of which he discovered Esther. Esther was everything he desired. Without so much as a "what for," she entered the king's harem and came only when she was called.

Prior to becoming queen, Esther had lived under dubious circumstances with her cousin Mordecai, who served as her guardian. Mordecai, a Jew, not only encouraged his orphaned cousin to marry a pagan king, he also instructed her to hide her Jewish identity. When, as a result of Mordecai's failure to bow before him, the king's advisor Haman obtained royal approval for his plot to kill all the Jews, Mordecai reversed his instructions to Esther. He implored his cousin to risk her life on behalf of her people.

Esther obeyed her cousin and humbled herself before the king. Mercifully, he heard her plea. The king declared that he could not rescind the royal decree against the Jews, but he did order Haman's death and allowed the Jews to take up arms. The resulting conflict caused much bloodshed. The Jews killed 800 men in Shushan alone and another 75,000 in the provinces. (No mention is made in the megillah of any Jewish casualties.) At Esther's bidding, they also impaled the ten sons of Haman to ensure that they could not avenge their father's death.

And so the Jews were saved, and there was much rejoicing and gladness. Mordecai and Esther undertook to record this story, so that it might be known for generations to come.

Told this way, it is a disturbing tale, no? And yet a close reading of the Megillah of Esther will reveal that all of this - and a few other unsavory things I neglected to mention - is in fact part of the story. Beyond the apparent license it provides us to rejoice at the death of our enemies, the Megillah also appears to sanction drunkenness, violence, and female oppression. Because of this, some liberal Jews have suggested that we not observe

Purim at all.

I think that their concern is clearly justifiable. But I also believe that the Purim dilemma can be resolved in a different way.

I mentioned before that there are observances connected with Purim which have failed to capture our attention. One of these observances is called Shabbat Zachor - the Sabbath of Remembrance. Shabbat Zachor is the special name we give to the Sabbath just before Purim. It is an occasion for us to remember the oppression which Jews have suffered - not only the deeds of the Haman recorded in the Scroll of Esther, but the deeds of all the other "Hamans" of our history (the Egyptian pharaoh who enslaved us; Amalek, who made war on the wandering Israelites by attacking them from behind; the Grand Inquisitor of Spain, the cruel czars of Russia, and Hitler).

Shabbat Zachor also comes to remind us that we are not alone in our suffering - indeed, we ourselves are guilty of bringing suffering to others. While we have often been the object of persecution, we as a people are not altogether innocent of bloodshed.

The day preceding Shabbat Zachor is also a day of remembrance, and it too has a special name: Ta'anit Esther, the Fast of Esther. In the megillah, Esther declares a fast because she fears her people will be annihilated, and because she hopes that her repentance will awaken God's mercy and help her to save her people.

For those who may find some of the messages of Purim objectionable, this fast might continue to serve a purpose - the purpose of displaying the wisdom and sensitivity of our faith. In Judaism, joy is always tempered by sorrow - a truth symbolized by the glass which is always broken under the wedding chuppah, and by the drops of wine we remove from our cups as we count out the Ten Plagues at our seder.

Too often, Reform Judaism has been accused of

ignoring tradition to serve its own purposes, to make Judaism more "convenient" for people to observe, or to make it more comfortable, so that it resonates more to our modern sensibilities.

But to deprive ourselves of Purim is tantamount to throwing the baby out with the bathwater. Our tradition itself provides us with the means to assuage any guilt we might incur by reading the story of Esther. More than that, the Fast of Esther and Shabbat Zachor serve to temper what would otherwise seem to be unmitigated joy at the fall of an enemy - an emotion that runs contrary to Jewish morality of any era.

For centuries, Purim has held an important place in the hearts of the Jewish people. The story of Esther and Mordecai has served to remind us of the eternal resilience of our people. In the face of persecution and despair, Purim has inspired us with hope and renewed our faith.

Maimonides wrote this:

> In messianic times all the Prophetic Books and Writings will cease to be used, except for the book of Esther. For this will continue to endure, just as the five books of the Law and the rules of the Oral Law will never be rescinded. And so, although all memory of ancient troubles will disappear ... the days of Purim will not cease to be observed. (Mishnah Torah, chapter 2)

And as it is said in the megillah of Esther (9:28), "And these days of Purim should not fail among the Jews, nor the memorial of them perish from their seed."

We need not cross Purim off our list of holidays. We need only to be reminded to temper our joy, to remember that the world is a less than perfect place, and that where there is room for joy, there is room for sorrow also.

Drawing by Susan Friesen

Rabbi Cheryl Rosenstein
December 21, 1991 4 Tevet, 5751
Shabbat Vayigash
Mount Zion Temple, St. Paul

Ritual, Tradition and Fellow Seekers

Two weeks ago, a local rabbi told the press that the current Lubavitch rebbe, Menachem Mendel Schneerson, is the messiah. This week, the front page of the *Star Tribune's* "Variety" section carried a story about a new book entitled *Spirituality in Children*. The cover story of a recent issue of *Life* magazine was devoted to the subject, "Who Is God?" And the latest edition of the locally-produced "reader's digest of alternative journalism," the "*Utne Reader*," also focused on the theme of spirituality.

Never mind the fall of Jimmy, Tammy, and the Electronic Church. Never mind that Mother Theresa has entered retirement. Religion is making a comeback in America.

Those of you who were raised in the tradition of what we call "Classical Reform" may be alarmed to learn that Jews and Judaism are taking part in the renaissance. Thirty percent of my classmates in rabbinical school observe some form of *kashrut* (dietary laws). A colleague in Los Angeles is successfully encouraging her congregants to don *tallitot* and *kipot*. Rabbis are talking about God on the *bima*.

What is going on? Why, as we enter the 1990's, are we returning to religion?

Sociologists of religion liken the religious history of the United States to a pendulum which swings back and forth - from Puritan exclusiveness to democratic tolerance, from revival meetings to labor meetings, from "God lives" to "God is dead." But what is it that drives the pendulum? What is it that has caused us to move again toward affiliation and ritual observance, or at least toward open discussion of spiritual issues?

One of the articles in the *"Utne Reader"* was written by a man who considered himself a "nothing," that is, devoid of religious affiliation or identification. His wife was also raised without specific religious commitment. This was fine for all concerned, he says, until a house fire down the street killed his children's best playmates. Suddenly, the author needed to answer the question, "Why?" Why was the world so unjust that innocent children had to die in such a way? Where were these children now? In Heaven? With God?

A rabbi turned psychologist by the name of Edward Friedman observed that every life cycle event, whether joyous or mournful, is a crisis event. Every birth, every bar mitzvah, every wedding and every funeral constitutes a crisis in the life of a family. It is no coincidence that it is these events, more than any others, which bring alienated and unaffiliated persons back to their churches and synagogues. More people join synagogues in connection with life-cycle events than for any other reason.

Crisis is what brings people to religion. A house fire. A death. Things that raise a lot of Big Questions.

What about science? you ask. What about reason and rationality? What happened to those?

It's true that science and reason have taught us a lot about our world. We know how cells divide. We are learning how viruses operate. We can put satellites and telescopes and people into space. But the more we know, the more we learn what we don't know. We don't know what causes Sudden Infant Death Syndrome. We don't know how to cure AIDS. We haven't figured out a way to dispose of the dangerous chemicals and energy sources we've discovered. We don't even know how to reach a peaceful settlement with another human being so as to avoid having to go to war.

We don't know how to do these things. And we really

don't know why things are the way they are a lot of the time.

The newest scientific explanation of how the world works is called The Theory of Chaos. This theory proposes that things do not always occur in a predictable, organized pattern. A lot of what goes on in the world is totally random.

While science has provided a lot of answers, it has led us to discover a whole set of questions. Big questions. Ones we can't find the answers to. Our "information explosion" has become an "information crisis."

It's about a week too early for the media to begin their traditional year-end retrospectives, but when they do, the lists will include a good number of other kinds of crises: The continuation of the intifada. The Berlin Wall. The end of the Cold War and its aftermath. The Gulf Crisis. Add to this short list all the big things I left out, the ones that affect us as a country, and all the smaller, daily crises we face on a day-to-day basis, and I think we can see why we're all "getting religion" again. The rule of chaos has us running scared.

For the last several weeks we've been re-reading the story of Joseph. You remember - the guy with the Amazing Technicolor Dreamcoat, the kid who doesn't get along with his older brothers and ends up being thrown into a pit and then sold to a band of Ishmaelites who take him to Egypt and sell him into slavery.

The sages claim that Joseph's entire life was predestined, that his arrival in Egypt and subsequent rise to power were part of a Divine plan. It is possible to read Joseph's story in that way.

But we moderns don't believe in predestination. As Rabbi Akiba said, "Free will is given." We do not, cannot subscribe to the idea that people are pawns in Someone's game of chess.

I have said that religion is a product of crisis. Of all

the Biblical characters we meet in the book of Genesis, no one's life is more complicated and unpredictable than that of Joseph. His brothers betray him, his boss's wife has him thrown into prison, his father believes him to be dead. And yet Joseph, when faced with an opportunity to get even with his brothers, forgives them. "Do not be angry with yourselves," he says, "it is not you who sent me here, but God."

With this statement, Joseph is not only consoling his brothers. He is consoling himself - telling himself that his life has not been a random series of hapless events, but that it has served some Higher purpose.

Who Needs God? Harold Kushner asks this question in the title of his newly-published book. In this random, unpredictable, chaotic world, all of us do. "There are no atheists in foxholes," the saying goes. We turn to God - however we choose to define that concept - when we need help. When we need to make moral decisions, we turn to God for the answers. When we are weak and weary, we turn to God to help us find the inner strength we need to go on. When we cannot forgive ourselves for our mistakes, we turn to God for forgiveness.

All of us, at one time or another, seek the answer to one of life's big questions. All of us need the consolation that our lives are not lived in vain.

As long as these things are true about human beings, religion will continue to play a role in our lives. People will continue to find comfort in ritual and tradition, and in the company of fellow seekers.

There is an age-old story of a man who was lost in a forest. For days he walks in circles, unable to find his way out. And one day, he meets another man. "Thank God," he says, "I've been lost here in the forest for days! Can you tell me the way out?"

"No," the other replies, "I, too, have been lost here for some time. But I know this - the way I have gone is not the right way. Come, let us look for the way together."

Our lives and the life of the world around us seem to be governed by the rule of chaos. So regardless of our differences of opinion and even our different interpretations of who and what God is, my advice, my friends, echoes that of Robert Fulghum: "Let's hold hands and stick together."

Reverend Anne Miner Pearson

The Rev. Anne Miner-Pearson

Born: Kansas, City, Missouri
Religious Background: Episcopal; raised Disciples of Christ
Education: B.S. in Education, University of Kansas; M. Div., Seabury Western Theological Seminary (Outstanding Preaching award), 1983.
Employment: Rector of St. Anne's Episcopal Church, Sunfish Lake (liturgy, program development, pastoral care, education, administration); YWCA Minneapolis leader award, 1985; Founding Feminist award, Ramsey County chapter of Minnesota Women's Political Caucus, 1986; Interim Rector, St. Mary's Episcopal Church, St. Paul, 1984-86; Human Resource Specialist, IDS Financial Services; seventh grade world history teacher.
Personal: married to Daniel V. Pearson (Episcopal priest); children Sarah, 26, and Michael, 24
Hobbies and Interests: travel, cooking, physical fitness, reading, being with my extended family.

Her name is Elizabeth, and her story is briefly told in the beginning of Luke's gospel.

Wife of a temple priest, Elizabeth miraculously becomes pregnant in her old age. Her hill country home is also where her young kinswoman, Mary of Nazareth, spends the first month of an even more miraculous motherhood. Through Elizabeth's word of greeting to Mary, Luke proclaims the Christian belief in the Lordship of Mary's Son. Imagination must suffice for the rest of their conversations and their understanding of God's presence in their lives.

However, before Elizabeth leaves the gospel story, Luke includes one more incident: the naming of Elizabeth's son at his circumcision. Those at the gathering expect the child to be named Zechariah after his father. Elizabeth, with what must have been great courage, speaks in opposition.

She pushes against tradition, declares her wishes for the future, and *forms* that future by claiming the power to name. Her son is to be called John. Once that power has been executed, her husband Zechariah is again able to speak, having been silenced by God nine months before. Out of the silence of male tradition comes the validation of the female voice for the future.

Her name is Elizabeth and mine is Anne. Her home in the hills of Judea is in stark contrast to mine in midwestern, middle-class America. Yet, her story has framed my understanding of my ministry.

Like Elizabeth, I was older when I received a call from God that radically changed how I would live my life. From the world of the suburban household, I started on a journey that took me back to school after twenty years, meant a move from Minneapolis to Chicago, and took me through a four-year process ending with ordination as an Episcopal priest.

In many ways, my preparation for ordination was like a pregnancy late in life. There was wonder and joy, a sense of the miracle that was happening to me. Interwoven with those feelings was a sense of burden and labor. Seminary classes, internship, diverse commitments, spiritual doubts, all took the physical strength demanded in carrying an unborn child. I often felt too old. I imagine Elizabeth did, too.

I also imagine Elizabeth welcoming Mary, the bearer of Jesus. An inviting space behind her, Elizabeth stands at the door in my imagination. Her hands extend in a warm touch. Her ears are ready to listen. She waits to be one with the woman who enters with the seeds of God. She greets with words that affirm the holiness and fruit of her visitor.

That picture of Elizabeth has become an icon of hope for my ministry. I serve as first pastor of a growing congregation formed in 1985 by the merger of two dying ones. Different traditions, ages and visions of the future of the Church combine to create a diverse mix among the members. Like Elizabeth, I encourage an open space where each member's perspective is heard and valued. For me, such an open space consists of the time and opportunity where we can stand together, even in our differences. Our common search for God deserves room to question, explore, evaluate, and celebrate.

Because I believe that everyone, like Mary, comes bearing God in their bodies and in their lives, stories are important to me. One service each Sunday ends with my inviting the youngest members to gather around me to hear a story relating to that day's readings. Of course, the older members unashamedly eavesdrop. But best of all, I like to hear and tell personal stories. Both the imaginary tale of a three-year-old and the twists of a life lived 82 years renew my delight and awe at God's children.

I am endlessly blessed by others' willingness to talk to me from their heads and hearts. I can understand Jesus' use of story as a way to see with new eyes. My hope, as I listen to my own and others' stories, is that God in me may stir a recognition and affirmation of God in them.

Of all the many and varied aspects of parish ministry, it is sermon preparation that most stirs the unborn seeds of God in me. Study, prayer, thinking and conversations that help me discern the theme of each sermon are both the most difficult and rewarding parts of any week, and they only bring me to the hardest task of all: writing the sermon. Early in my ordained ministry, a colleague spoke of this whole process as a pregnancy leading to the birth at the end of the week! I find that an apt metaphor.

On a Friday morning, when I face my word processor screen, I know that an experience of giving birth is ahead. There is the labor, sometimes easy and short; other times, long and arduous. Also surprises are bound to appear. I'd like to believe that those surprises are God's mysterious

Spirit working anew, in spite of all the scholars' opinions and my own ideas of what to say. So when Sunday morning comes, I join the others in offering the best of the week to God, trusting God's acceptance, and hoping that its message will spiritually feed at least one.

Finally, Elizabeth's story gives me courage in my ministry. I see her bravely assuming the role of naming which traditionally belongs to others. She is not silent as others often wish women would be. She speaks out. I want such a bold voice to be part of my ministry. I model her courage when I question procedures which disrespect another's privacy or piece of truth. Her story nudges me to suggest alternatives to what has always been done in the name of a tradition which has narrowly defined ministry and spiritual experience.

From Elizabeth's story, I know that God calls women, even older women, to speak of what we know and hope for the future. The words we speak and the lives we lead will hopefully free the tongues of our traditions, promoting the health and wholeness of the entire community.

Rev. Anne Miner-Pearson
St. Anne's Episcopal Church
Sunfish Lake, Minnesota
December 24, 1987
Luke 2:1-14

Swaddling God

Twenty Christmases ago, I had just given birth to my second and last child.

Although each birth is always uniquely different, recovery from this birth followed the pattern of those days. Gone were the lengthy hospital stays known by my mother's generation, with its two-week regimen of bed rest, short careful walks, and babies cared for mainly by nurses in the nursery down the hall. I was ordered up by the next day and Michael was brought into my room for every feeding - although the diaper changing, thankfully, was handled by others! After four days, I was back home.

Twenty years later as I return to the maternity wards as a visitor, I notice that the changes have continued. These days we friends and clergy must act quickly after receiving the news of the child's arrival. A day or two of delay will find us at the information desk hearing that the mother and baby have already gone home. And for the baby, the short stay means almost no time in the hospital's nursery. Instead, the newborn has slept (or not slept as the case may be) right in Mom's room - only it's no longer just Mom's room. It's also Dad's room, and siblings have been in and out, lounging around in a room that resembles a spacious motel suite.

Those are the obvious changes, but there is another one that I noticed but didn't think too much about until I reread one line in the familiar Christmas story we just heard: "And she gave birth to her first-born son and wrapped him in swaddling cloths." And then I remembered the newborn babies I'd held recently and what must be the current "baby-wrapping" method. My babies were wrapped, certainly, but not like those born these days. These babies are really wrapped! The blanket is tucked around the tiny body; the ends disappear into the folds until the bundle resembles a cocoon. No arm or leg free to kick off the covers, no finger left exposed to the cold air. Contained. Safe. Protected. Bound. Wrapped like I think Mary's first-born son Jesus was wrapped on the night he was born, only his blanket was long, narrow bands of cloth that circled his body.

And isn't Mary's action understandable? What parent wouldn't want her child to be safe, contained, and warm, especially when the birth was far from home and occurred in a strange place? What parent wouldn't attempt to create a space safe from the cold blast of the world?

But it's not just parents who know this urge to contain, protect and bind. Surely it is all of us. All of us can understand Mary's response to hold close what is cherished. The world is full of danger and pain: the car speeding down the street, the cruel comment of a friend, the loss of a job, the body trapped in pain and decay, the threat of nuclear destruction. There is much to fear and many reasons to hold close, to protect what we already know, to maintain the familiar.

Mary's swaddling of her baby reminds us of this part of ourselves. We wrap *our* swaddling cloths to cover our loneliness. We tuck in our feelings of inadequacy so they can never be seen - just our defensive, curt retort gives any clue. We fold our fear under the softness of denial. We pull our ragged ends tightly around ourselves until we think no one could guess what our smooth exterior covers.

And our relationship with God does not escape swaddling either. Just as we bind ourselves, so we bind God. We want our God small and easy to hold on to, a God who can be understood and related to in simple terms. We pray for what we want and expect God, the magician, to provide it. Or God is some gigantic police spirit waiting until we make a mistake, take the wrong step, utter a harmful word. Then God taps our conscience, nudges our guilt, and urges us to make up for it. Or perhaps God is this pappy, saccharin and sweet so as not to be taken seriously at our mature stage of life - all right for children and simple folk, but of no significance in the parts of our lives that really matter.

Tuck in the ends, fold over the excess, tighten up the circle. Swaddle God.

But if we believe what we proclaim this night, that the first-born child of Mary was also God and came from God to save us from brokenness, loneliness and death, then as she wrapped the child, wasn't Mary swaddling God? Wasn't Mary binding up, *containing* God? Without the rest of the sentence, it might seem that way. But the story goes on: "And she laid him in a manger." What a contrast! She carefully protects her child and then places him in the strangest of all cribs: a manger, an earthy, common trough designed to feed another, belonging to another. She courageously releases her child, the child who will grow to most fully reveal God's promise of peace and love, this child who is both human and divine.

So, was Mary binding God? No, not possible. Not possible for her and not possible for us, for God *will be* in the manger. God will be in the world, in a space we would not choose to find the Holy Other, in a space that doesn't belong to us. God will work *through* our swaddling cloths, our narrow and confined view of God and of ourselves. God is prepared to be in our world, however untimely or bizarre the arrival may seem, however limited God may be perceived. God arrives anyway ....

As we proclaim this night, God sometimes arrives as a small, new sign of life, as fragile and vulnerable as a new-born baby. God is that tiny spark of love that promises a new beginning in a relationship declared dead. God is the tenuous resolve to try again when the pain and disappointment cry: "Withdraw." "Isolate."

Or sometimes God pushes through our wrappings as the challenge of the adult Jesus. He no longer resides in the manger; now he speaks in marketplace and home. He calls for commitment, discipleship. He points to the stranger and calls us to care. He points to an enemy and calls us to love. He overturns our world of order and control until our questions are more numerous than our answers.

He grows from a tightly-wrapped baby in a manger hidden in a tiny hillside village to a power and love so strong and open that finally he is not bound at all. He hangs stretched wide on a cross outside the politically important town of Jerusalem. There is nothing left to hide. There is nothing left to say. God has been seen. God has pushed aside the swaddling cloths. Brokenness, loneliness, and death are seen undisguised.

If we dare to look, we can see why we want to hide. It is not a pretty sight. A baby in a manger has much more appeal than a broken body on a cross. But if we dare to look at God unbound, we will find a God whose power and love for us knows no bounds, not even the bounds of death. It is this God who yearns to break into our lives this Christmas night, inviting us to hold God close, protected and safe, while also knowing that what we hold this night, or at any other time, is only a small, tightly bound grasp of God. Like a new-born baby, it is only a beginning. But we can hold on to that.

Drawing by Susan Friesen

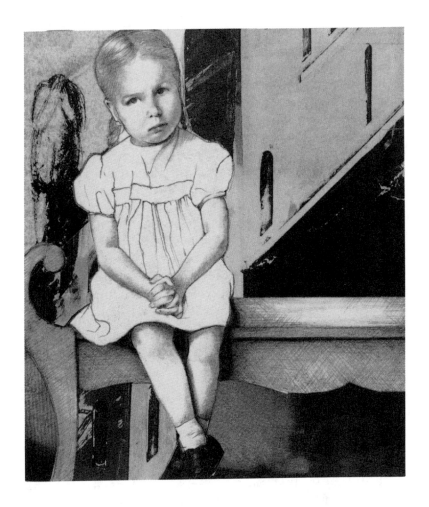

The Rev. Anne Miner-Pearson
St. Anne's Episcopal Church, Sunfish Lake
Second Sunday after Epiphany, 1989
John 2:1-11

A Stone Jar

I stood off to one side, not really part of the festivities. Tall, strong and regal, I knew my place. I knew my role and now was not the time nor the place for my task. I understood such demarcation. That's the way life should be, divided into departments and roles. That way everything and everyone could best perform their allotted tasks. Taking turns according to the decided pattern prevented any disputes about who does what and when. I liked life like that.

So I really didn't mind standing apart from the celebration, for I was a large stone jar, a household vessel of sunbaked clay, shaped and sculpted. I didn't mind my emptiness, for when I was needed for the purification rites, I would be filled. I was used to feeling that emptiness and had rather accepted it as a necessary part of knowing my place in the system.

True, sometimes I wished I could be full more often, to feel that cool, clear water splashing into my emptiness, filling me to the top, that exciting feeling that I was needed, that I contained the stuff of life, that I held a precious gift for others. But most of the time, I stood on the side and tried not to remember and hope. To be satisfied that I was used at all, to understand my place and accept it.

I did hear a strange conversation that day of the wedding, though. It was between a young man and apparently his mother. They were guests, but you would never have known it by the way he took charge of the situation. It was like he was the host, not an invited guest.

And the way he answered his mother was as much of a flipflop. First he rebuked her for trying to involve him in the problem of no wine, and then he became the obedient son who did as she expected.

But I quickly forgot about her because all of a sudden I was no longer on the sidelines, watching the celebration. At his command, I was brought into the center of the activity of getting more wine. It was not the right time, mind you, and I hardly knew how to behave. Then I felt it - the water reaching down into my depths - the wonderful stream of life filling me up. Not the right time or place, I knew, but how marvelous to be taken by surprise, to have my deepest need fulfilled, quite by surprise, quite out of turn, quite out of time.

The water filled me to the brim. Oh, I was afraid they would not stop in time and I would overflow, spilling over into the world around me. But they did stop in time and I stood in wonder and awe at my new state.

I had been at the sidelines
Now I was part of the feast.
I had been empty
Now I was full.

All this happened at the command of that young man, because he was there.

Then he spoke again: "Now draw some out, and take it to the steward of the feast." "No," I wanted to cry. "Don't take any out. I have only started to enjoy the unexpected blessing of being filled. Besides, it's not the right time and the right place for my contents to be used. It's all wrong. It's not by the rules."

But with his command to share with others, something inside of me stirred. Because he stood by, I was changed. Not on the outside, for I still stood tall and regal, a stone jar. But inside, inside, things were different. The water became more than just the stuff of life. It became the celebration of life, the laughter and blessing of all of life.

My urge to hold back was gone. My fear that I would overflow became the desire to do just that - to spill what I felt and held inside so that all the world would know what the presence of that man had given to me. I wanted to share, to offer myself, to pass on the change that had happened in me. I ached for the stewards to dip into my plenty and carry it to those who had been without, to fill those who knew emptiness that they might know what it was to be filled - the surprise, the wonder, the mystery.

He had spoken to me and such an event had transformed my life. Because of him, my life was more whole. Water could mix with wine for all was a gift from him. More than I had even hoped for was now possible. I, who had only seen myself as separate from the whole, as only intended for one purpose, could become the bearer of the feast, the proclaimer of his presence.

I knew that eventually all that I held would be consumed, for wine not shared becomes bitter and sour. I would become an empty vessel again. Yet there was something about his presence and his power that brought hope and trust. He would fill my jar again, for he desired that it be so.

> *With Jesus, there was the sense that life was*
> *more than we expected,*
> *more than we deserved,*
> *more than we could earn.*
> *Life was the best.*

Rabbi Stacy K. Offner

Rabbi Stacy K. Offner

Born: New York, New York
Religious Background: Jewish
Education: B.A. Magna Cum Laude in Religion, Kenyon College, 1977; M.A. in Hebrew Literature, Hebrew Union College, 1982; ordained, Hebrew Union College, 1984; Green Prize in Midrash and Hebrew, 1982; Steinberg Memorial Prize, 1983.
Personal: partner Nancy Abramson, social worker; stepchildren Jill, 18 and Charlie, 16.
Employment: Rabbi, Shir Tikvah Congregation, St. Paul (worship, preaching, teaching, counseling, religious school; adjunct professor at Hamline University; formerly Associate Rabbi at Mount Zion Temple (St. Paul).
Interests, hobbies: exploring new cities, visiting in cafes, reading great books, driving back roads, walking the lakes.

I never considered myself a very religious person. I grew up in New York where the presumption (at least on my part!) was that *everyone* was Jewish. Because everyone was Jewish, I never could understand any stereotypes about Jews. My friends had all sorts of different kinds of physical appearances, my friends had all sorts of different kinds of personalities, my friends had all sorts of different kinds of dreams for their futures.

Other than a brief moment in second grade when I adored my science teacher (I came home from school one day that year and announced that I was going to be a "human bythologist" when I grew up, just like my science teacher who actually happened to be a marine biologist), I don't recall ever dreaming to be anything other than a rabbi, a dream which first entered my psyche when I was about 15 years old.

My desire to be a rabbi had nothing to do with God. I don't think I considered matters of faith to be very primary to me at that time. (Though I sure was drawn to the religious services that, as high school students, we wrote and observed as a peer group and I found deeply meaningful. At that point in my life, I was more aware of the shivers that occasionally ran down my spine at a peak moment in the service rather than any God ... can God speak to us in the form of shivers?)

The most exciting thing about Judaism was and still is the intellectual challenge and stimulation that it provides. It was when I was 15 that I had the good fortune of first meeting Rashi, a brilliant medieval scholar whose vast commentaries on the Bible and the Talmud are still regarded as the foremost commentaries of the day and are studied today by all serious students of Judaism. Studying Judaism probed my mind - and the furthermost recesses of my soul.

Just as important as Rashi are the people who introduced me to him. Judaism is never studied in isolation. I thank God for all my teachers, who were themselves exemplary students of Judaism. I think of those teachers and admire them for their erudition, their integrity, their passion about justice, and their commitment to humanity (read: me). I feel humbled by my recollection of them, but it is truly my deepest desire to have my rabbinate permeated with those same ideals: erudition, integrity, passion about justice and commitment to humanity.

My first trip to Israel also had incredible impact. I spent six months living and working on a kibbutz while also attending classes at the University of Haifa. The kibbutz and the university were two simultaneous enactments of Judaism. At school we would study the ancient texts about a land flowing with milk and honey, and on the kibbutz we would pick grapefruit. At school we would study about the fundamental essence of community life, and on the kibbutz we would each contribute to the welfare of the whole. Walking through Jerusalem was returning to a home I never knew I had been to before. The prayers that emanated from the stone wall of the Second Temple were prayers that emanated through me. My forebears bequeathed to me the wisdom of the years and I rejoice at the possibility of gleaning from that wisdom as we face the peculiarities and challenges of our modern day.

I love being a rabbi. Oh, there more mundane activities than I had envisioned, but on the other side of the spectrum, I would have to say that the miracles are beyond my wildest dreams. It is a privilege to walk through life's most exhilarating and tragic and intimate moments with the people who comprise my congregation. It is a privilege to be able to teach, to preach, to awaken people to more Jewish lives and as a result, to live lives that are enriched by two thousand years of tradition, a tradition that demands inquiry into the vast network of human behavior and its implications for the world in which we live.

Funny thing - but perhaps "human bythologist" is not that far off. It is the task of the biologist to plummet the depths of life itself. So too, being a rabbi demands of me an acute consciousness of the world around us. Judaism provides for me - and for my congregation - a magnificent guide for walking through our magnificent world.

Rabbi Stacy Offner
August 2, 1985

The Rabbi's Sister

In her efforts to imagine what women would have been like, and what kind of literature they would have produced, Virginia Woolf embarks upon a fanciful discourse of what Shakespeare's sister would have been like ... had Shakespeare had a sister.

Let's imagine, she writes, what would have happened had Shakespeare had a wonderfully gifted sister, called Judith, let us say. Shakespeare himself went, very probably, to the grammar school, where he learned Latin and the elements of grammar and logic. He had a taste for theater, became a successful actor, and lived at the hub of the universe, meeting everybody, practicing his art, and exercising his wit.

Meanwhile his extraordinarily gifted sister, let us suppose, remained at home. She was as adventurous, as imaginative, as anxious to see the world as he was. But she was not sent to school. She had no chance of learning grammar and logic, let alone of reading Latin.

She had the quickest fancy, a gift like her brother's, for the tune of words. Like him, she had a taste for the theater. She took the road to London one night, and stood at the stage door. She wanted to act, she said. Men laughed in her face. The manager scoffed at her. She could get no training for her craft.

Totally thwarted, she finally killed herself one winter's night and lies buried at some cross-road where the buses now run.

Who is to say if Virginia Woolf's scenario is likely to have been true or likely to have been false? What is truly significant to me, is not in Virginia Woolf's story, but in her need to tell it. Woolf needed to create a woman where one did not exist; to imagine a woman's story that was not handed down to us.

Our sermon series this summer is on Famous Rabbis. And that means, among other things, a series of sermons about Famous Men. Now I know as well as anyone that there's such a thing as a woman rabbi - but thirteen years of ordaining women rabbis, and less than a hundred of us in the world as yet, hardly makes for much "Famous Rabbi" material.

The title "rabbi" has been in use now for over 2,000 years. When we speak of Rabbi So-and-so or Rabbi So-and-so, we may be referring to a rabbi who lived a thousand years ago, a hundred years ago, or yesterday. But when we talk about "The Rabbis" or "The Period of the Rabbis," we are talking about the rabbis who lived during the time of the Talmud. And that means rabbis who lived from around the year 0 through the year 500.

And as important as it is for Virginia Woolf to will into being a female counterpart to Shakespeare, so do I wonder what it would have been like if "The Rabbis" had sisters. And that's where we are just a little bit luckier than Virginia Woolf. Because The Rabbis did have sisters. And we even know a little about them - or at least - about one of them.

Bruriah lived in the second century, during the revolt of Bar Kochba, that last and ill-fated attempt of the Jews to free themselves from Roman rule in the year 135 of the Common Era. Her wisdom and righteousness were legendary even in her own time. She is the only woman in Talmudic times whose views were not only recorded in the Talmud, but helped to shape Jewish law. Bruriah was also a teacher in the academy - a pretty remarkable status for a Jewish woman in 135!

What kind of woman must Bruriah have been? Where did she learn so much? How was she able to teach? And what must it have been like for her, to live at a time when, though her genius was recognized, it must have been considered a bit freakish?

We don't know who taught Bruriah how to read, or how she came to be an avid student of Torah. But I think it is no coincidence that she came from a rabbinic family, and probably learned much of what she knew within the setting where women were permitted - the family home.

Bruriah was the daughter of a rabbi and the wife of the very important Rabbi Meir. For Bruriah to take part in the discussions and debates of the rabbis was, for her, probably an easy extension of what she grew up with around her kitchen table. In one such debate over a very technical matter of ritual purity, she found herself head to head with her own brother. At the conclusion of the argument, the rabbis claimed: "The daughter has answered more correctly than the son." Bruriah's brother, overshadowed and humiliated by the prowess of his sister, never did amount to very much. (Thank goodness, I suppose, that Shakespeare never did have a sister!)

What we know of Bruriah - who she was and what she believed in - comes to us by way of the Talmud. Some stories in the Talmud make reference to her, others tell tales about her, and all speak very highly of her as a student, as a teacher, and as a woman.

We know that Bruriah was an excellent student and that she apparently went through the intensive three-year course of study customary for disciples of rabbis at that time. Her reputation as a brilliant student was so great that it spawned legends about her studiousness.

The story is written in the Talmud that Rabbi Simlai came before Rabbi Yohanan and proposed the masterful Rabbi Yohanan teach him the Book of Genealogies in a three-month course of study. Thereupon Rabbi Yohanan took a clod of earth and threw it at him, saying, "If Bruriah, the wife of Rabbi Meir and daughter of Rabbi Hananya, who studies three hundred laws from three hundred teachers in one day, could not complete the task in three years, how can you dare propose to do it in three months!"

Legend tells also of Bruriah's abilities as a teacher, and her particular style of teaching. One day she found a young man studying silently, not making the customary sounds, whereupon she said to him:

> "Is it not written: 'Ordered in all things and sure?' If it is ordered in your 248 limbs, it will be sure, otherwise, it will not be sure."

This quotation reflects the general attitude that learning was aided by the voice and the body, as well as by the mind. Bruriah not only taught the student a lesson, but did so in a particularly rabbinic fashion; she quoted from the Torah and argued her position by explaining and applying the scriptural passage. Her rebuke of the student was gentle; she tried to lead him more deeply into his studies.

Bruriah was not beyond chastising her rabbinic peers in a more scathing fashion, however, particularly when the issue was sensitive to her, as were all the laws that pointed to the inferior status of women. A famous example of this is recorded in a conversation she had with Rabbi Yosi. In it, she subtly and deftly pokes fun at the men who held prejudices against her sex.

Rabbi Yosi the Galilean was once on a journey when he met Bruriah. "By what road," he asked her," do we go to Lydda?" "Foolish Galilean!" she replied. "Did not the sages say 'Engage not in much talk with women?' You should have asked: 'By which to Lydda?'"

Once again, Bruriah uses a rabbinic style to make her point. Yet Bruriah never had the privilege of being called "rabbi." And we can only imagine what pain it caused her, to be denied access into the ranks of those with whom she studied, and whom she taught. Virginia Wolf imagines that Shakespeare's sister killed herself because she was closed out of the world that she so desperately sought. A little melodramatic, we might think, except when we turn and see that Bruriah did, in the end, take her own life. Why? We don't know. Again, as with so much of woman's experiences of the past, we can only imagine.

But what we know for sure, is that Bruriah was a brilliant student and teacher of Torah. She taught and lived an intensely moral life, and she was worthy of being addressed as Rabbi. And so on this Shabbat evening, 1800 years after she lived, she finds her way into a sermon series on Famous Rabbis. "Zichrona L'vracha." May her memory be a blessing.

Drawing by Susan Friesen.

Rabbi Stacy K. Offner
Congregation Shir Tikvah
Rosh Hashanah 5752
September 8, 1991

"Those Who Sow in Violence..."

Once a week, the newspaper sports a quiz that tests you on your knowledge regarding the major events of the past week. I always enjoy playing the game. I enjoy identifying the famous photographs: this week of Boris Yeltsin, last week of Mikhail Gorbachev. I usually find it tougher to answer the geographical questions - just where is Uzbekistan in relation to Kirghizia? Oh yes, I know, it was the Beach Boys who performed at the Grand Stand at the State Fair, and it is the city of St. Paul where the Human Rights Ordinance is once again up for grabs.

I wonder sometimes just who it is that writes that trivia quiz. I wonder if they would ever allow for write-in questions from the public. If they did, I know what mine would be. I would ask: How many times has Amalek appeared in the news this past week? The answer would be multiple choice. A. 2; B. 20; C. 200; D. More than the above. The answer, to those of us who know Amalek well, would be obvious: D. More times than we could possibly count.

Amalek first made his appearance back in Biblical days, for he was a contemporary of Moses. Historically speaking, he is virtually insignificant. A small bandit who attacked and looted nomadic peoples as they travelled through the desert. The Jews had certainly encountered far greater enemies than Amalek - great kings and pharaohs, to name just a few. So it is with much curiosity that we learn that in his last great speech to the Jews, just before they are about to enter the Promised Land, Moses, while pleading with them to do right and follow God's laws, leaves them with one final warning. It is not, as we might expect, a warning about Pharaohs to come. It is, rather, a warning about Amalek. Moses says:

"Remember what Amalek did to you on your journey, after you left Egypt - how, undeterred by fear of God, he surprised you on the march, when you were famished and weary, and he cut down all the stragglers in your rear. Therefore, when Adonai your God grants you safety from all your enemies around you, in the land that Adonai your God is giving you as an inheritance, you shall blot out the memory of Amalek from under heaven. Do not forget!"

It is not Pharaoh, but Amalek, that we have to worry about. For it was not Pharaoh, but Amalek, who attacked from the rear. The strongest members of the desert bands would march in the front, the weaker ones, in the rear. Undeterred by "fear of God," Amalek attacked the rear, the weakest portion of the band. Moses warns us to remember that there will always be an Amalek, an enemy who does not play by the rules.

Amalek has reared his ugly head again. And he is on the rise. Amalek appeared over a thousand times in the state of Minnesota just this past year in the form of a rapist. In 1978, 800 rapes were reported in Minnesota. That's more than two reported rapes, every day. Last year, the Minnesota Bureau of Criminal Apprehension documented 1445 reported rapes, or four rapes every day. In the rural areas of Minnesota, 78 rapes were reported in 1978. By 1987, there was more than a 300 percent increase in reported rapes in greater Minnesota.

By the middle of the summer of 1988, the Minnesota Poll reported that two-thirds of all women in the Twin Cities metropolitan area had restricted their activities or armed themselves to try to protect themselves from violent sexual assault. More than half of the women changed the place where they parked, or waited for someone to accompany them before going to their car. One in seven armed themselves with weapons or mace. Three out of ten citizens said they had become more afraid to go downtown. Of those who had become more fearful, 89 percent were women.

The statistics also have names. Kathleen Bullman, Angela Green and Angeline Whitebird-Sweet were found sexually mutilated, beaten and murdered at the hand of a single perpetrator.

Carrie Conrood, a nineteen-year-old student on her way to a job interview, was raped and stabbed to death in a downtown Minneapolis parking lot. Her alleged killer was a convicted sex offender who had recently been released from prison.

Melissa Johnson was walking her dog in her St. Cloud neighborhood and she never came home again.

Mary Foley was raped and strangled by a repeat sex offender in the parking ramp of her employer. The murderer admitted that he had sexually assaulted eight women in a period of one month's time. He killed Mary, the last of his many victims.

Steven Hicks had the misfortune of hitch-hiking, and accepting a ride from a stranger in 1978. The stranger turned out to be Jeffrey Dahmer, and Steven Hicks became the first victim of what, thirteen years later, we would discover to be one of the most horrific strings of slayings in modern times.

Eight-year-old Margaret Marques tells her mother that she is going to the bathroom in a Minneapolis discount store, and disappears.

John Chenoweth, former state senator and public servant, is shot to death just weeks ago because he loved men instead of women.

In Grand Rapids, Michigan, some people call the district courthouse the Carol Irons Hall of Justice. That is where Carol Irons became the first female judge in Kent County. That is also where she married a police officer two years later. And that is where she was shot to death in her chambers by her estranged husband.

The newspapers and the television news reports are unrelenting. The *Star-Trib* even saw fit to run a feature story on the newscasters themselves, and how they cope with the barrage of violence in today's world. Sadly, Don Shelby was quoted as saying: "You can't afford to absorb the grief or all the bad news that you have to report in a given night. You would not be able to carry your weight home. You would not be able to be a good father or husband."

Well, our job on this evening of Rosh Hashanah, IS to absorb it. We cannot turn our heads any longer. It is time to take a stand.

A survey of seventy-two ninth grade students in Carlton County, Minnesota, was presented to the Attorney General's Task Force on the Prevention of Sexual Violence Against Women. In this survey, more than half of the students agreed with the statement: "Rape victims are often weak and passive." Eighty-six percent of the students agreed that, "sexual assault can't really happen to you, if you don't want it to."

No wonder that Thelma and Louise became legendary folk heroes among the women in this country this summer! It is time to take a stand.

We are outraged by the violence perpetrated by men against women. We are outraged by the violence of heterosexual men against gay men. And most of all, we are outraged by the violence perpetrated by supposed adults against children.

Clearly, our Jewish faith demands that we always be outraged by the violence inflicted by the powerful against the powerless, by the oppressor against the oppressed. It is Amalek, and we are commanded to remember him.

But then a Chasidic Jew driving through the streets of Brooklyn accidently hits a seven-year-old black boy and knocks him over dead. A tragedy, to be sure. The rage bubbles up in the Black community. "Kill 'em for it! Kill 'em all!" And an innocent Jewish man is stabbed to death in retaliation for the accidental but fatal automobile excursion.

Where are we, as once again the lines are drawn between good and evil, between "us" and "them," between the oppressor and the oppressed? Who is the victim? And who the villain?

We stand by the Black community whose rage against societal injustice is so, so justified. We stand by the Black teenagers in our community who can't go outside and play ball in the streets without seeing white people react to them by clutching their purses. We stand by the Black parents who have to teach their innocent youngsters why people are afraid of them. We understand their rage.

But we also stand with our Jewish brothers and sisters who have too often been the target of a rage misguided.

Unemployment in Germany got you enraged? Blame the Jews! Victimization of the Palestinians by the entire Middle Eastern world got you enraged? Blame the Jews! Been inflicted with a plague or disease and you can't comprehend the cause? Blame the Jews!

In a violent world and a violent United States and a violent New York City and a violent Minnesota - one thing - and perhaps only one thing is for certain. There is enough rage in this world to go around tenfold.

We know that for certain. And we feel it, too. And the question is - what do we do with all our rage? Where do we place this powerful energy, this potential source of violence and destruction, that lies within us all?

The presence of evil in our world, especially that evil which is manifested in the form of violent acts perpetrated by the powerful against the powerless, has long anguished decent human beings world wide. What can we say of faith in the presence of such evil? What can we say of ethics in the presence of such evil? And what can we say to our own children, in the presence of such evil?

Judaism has long resisted the temptation to create a monolith out of evil. Evil is not a transcendent force out there and on the attack. Rather, evil - like good - is part of the life force that flows within us all. The rabbis called this impulse to do evil the *Yetzer Hara*.

This inclination to do evil is rooted deep inside of us, and is constantly struggling with our *Yetzer Hatov*, the inclination, also within us all, to do the right thing. The first death ever recorded in Biblical history was also a murder. When Cain killed his brother Abel, God protected Cain, and warned us: "If anyone kills Cain, Cain shall be avenged sevenfold." Violence begats violence. Those who sow in violence, reap in violence. It is time to break the cycle.

That is why in our Prayerbook this Rosh Hashanah we pray: "Adonai Eloheinu, Adonai our God, help us to overcome the impulse to do evil." Not them, but us. On these High Holidays our task is ourselves. We must make a beginning. And we must begin with ourselves. We must recognize our own anger, confront our own potential for violence, and turn that drive into constructive energy. Thelma's friend Louise never did confront her own anger. She never could tell Thelma or anyone else about the violent deed that had been perpetrated against her back in Texas. Instead, she became violent herself. Seven-fold, God warns us. Violence cannot be the response to violence.

When the Israelites were standing at the shore of the Red Sea, hemmed in behind by the chariots of Pharaoh and in front by the turbulent sea, the Midrash explains that at that moment of crisis there were four groups that offered counsel. The first group said: "We are lost. Let us plunge into the sea and die!" The second group said: "Let us return to slavery in Egypt." The third group said, "Let us raise our voices in protest to God." The fourth group said:

"With faith in God, let us go forward into the sea and advance to the Promised Land."

In the face of seemingly relentless evil, how tempting it is to be like the first group and yield to despair. We could also be like the second group and yield our freedom for the sake of security, but we will not. Nor will it be enough to be like the third group and petition and protest. But like the fourth group, we, too, will move forward.

We will move forward by first confronting our own evil impulses. We will move forward by protecting our children - not by protecting them from knowledge of the dangers in our world - but by educating them to recognize the danger signs and to strive themselves to do the right thing. We will move forward by speaking out at even the small violences we confront every day when we are treated with less respect and dignity than a human being deserves.

It is time to take a stand.

Reverend Judith M. Mattison

The Rev. Judith M. Mattison

Born: Milwaukee, Wisconsin
Religious Background: Lutheran
Education: B.S. Elementary Education, University of
Minnesota; M. Div., Luther Northwestern Seminary, St.
Paul, 1985; Charles E. Merrill Fellowship, Harvard Divinity
School, 1991.
Employment: Associate pastor, Mount Olivet Lutheran
Church, Minneapolis (pastoral care, preaching,
communications, director of Community Concern Board,
stewardship program, teaching); formerly program
director, Mount Olivet Retreat Center; educational
radio/television for Minneapolis Public Schools (writer,
producer, performer, editor); lay staff - communications,
stewardship and outreach ministries, Richfield Lutheran
Church; elementary school teacher; board member, Luther
Northwestern Seminary; Commission for Communications
Board chairperson for Evangelical Lutheran Church in
America; author of thirteen books published by Augsburg-
Fortress, Minneapolis.
Personal: divorced; children Theodore, 25, Michael, 23
Hobbies and Interests: tennis and dancing; strong
interests in the needs of children, the ecology of the
planet, and world hunger issues.

The call to ministry was, for me, a long process which
commenced with questions.

From early on I wondered about the purpose of life, the
meaning of suffering, and the presence of God. I might
well have gone to seminary after college, had there been
such an opportunity. As it was, it never entered my mind; I
had never known of a woman pastor.

I married a pastor and taught school and raised my two
sons. My children are very important to me. My ministry
took the form of writing, mostly books of devotions. There
I expressed my same questions and began to publicly shape

my theology and trust God's promises.

Shortly after my husband and I were separated, I entered seminary, largely on the urging of friends. Seminary was the place where I tested my faith and my sense of call. Ordained in 1985, I find ministry rewarding, interesting, exciting and nurturing.

My experiences in the church have included different kinds of settings: a small suburban church as a pastor's wife, larger churches as a member, and now a huge "megachurch" as a pastor.

Mount Olivet has about 13,000 members, with a pastoral staff of seven full-time pastors and a total staff of about 55 people. This is an unusual call, for the management of so large a church requires different skills and strengths. Each pastor has some measure of administration to do and we all do pastoral care (hospital calling, counseling, relationship building). The primary administration is in the hands of the senior pastor.

Mount Olivet Church has significant outreach ministries: a nursing home, a home for retired persons, a home for developmentally disadvantaged young people, a camp on the North Shore and a retreat center in Farmington, Minnesota. The pastors relate to all these places in various ways, with the primary management in the hands of directors and Boards.

The strength of Mount Olivet is its careful attention to three areas: pastoral care, youth and worship. Our traditional worship is necessarily well-organized, for we have four services each Sunday morning, with Holy Communion served each week at smaller services. Music is valued by our members.

Our youth are very important to us. They are treated with respect, and given guidance by an excellent and adequately large staff. The camping program helps to build the larger youth program, and there are excellent caring outreach programs in which many of our youth participate.

We have a storefront program for neighborhood youth who are at risk, as well as a full-time junior high program. Youth are not an afterthought, but important people at Mount Olivet.

Because of the size of the congregation, it is crucial that we provide opportunities for people to gather in smaller communities of common interest. Our adult education programs facilitate that superbly and they are very well attended. Our pastoral care department makes every effort to be in touch with hospitalized and shut-in members. I am assigned to hospitals and emergencies for a week at a time about once every six weeks. During those weeks, a pastor may visit as many as ten hospitals and some twenty to thirty-five members. It's a busy time!

Ministry at Mount Olivet is a very public ministry. People see us at some distance a large part of the time. We also see them in large groups, and all over the city or country - because there are so many of them! The sheer numbers can be a drain on one's emotional energy. However, people on the whole seem to understand our limitations and, for example, do not expect us to remember everyone's name at all times.

Part of the demand of such a ministry includes a schedule over which one has little control. When we have new member open houses, there are four or five of them; there are fifteen stewardship dinners which all pastors attend, plus luncheons and breakfasts; there are eight Easter and nine Christmas Eve services which all pastors participate in. It is a very public ministry.

My greatest love is preaching. It is in that process that I sort out my theology and explore my faith journey. I preach rather seldom at Mount Olivet, so I rely on my writing and a brief weekly radio program to help sustain me in lieu of full sermons. We also preach at our nursing home from time to time. Occasionally, I preach at other churches or events.

I work with a group of caring and professional colleagues. We are supportive of one another and there is a distinct lack of competitiveness. Each person is professional in his/her ministry work and we respect each other's particular competencies.

I consider language a crucial concern for anyone in ministry. We are all shaped by the words which are used to describe us. Inclusive language is a significant issue for anyone who preaches and teaches the Word of God. In steady, caring ways I hope to raise people's consciousness in regard to the power of language and the importance of each person's dignity being cherished as we speak of and to them. I look for the day when our whole society sees the value of inclusive language and uses it.

Of course, ministry can be frustrating. One can never accomplish all one has hopes of doing. On the other hand, it is a work of great satisfaction and wonderful affirmation! Mount Olivet is a place of considerable positive attitudes and I have benefitted from that general climate.

I'm grateful for the people who continue to inspire me: our refugee resettlement committee, the volunteers at our nursing home, the youth who relate to inner-city children, the believers who pray regularly for others.

My faith may never be fully "in place," but the Spirit of God works through these many people and the church and daily experiences to sustain me. I'm grateful for the challenge of ministry and I love my work! God is good.

The Rev. Judith M. Mattison
Mount Olivet Lutheran Church, Minneapolis
August 26, 1990
Matthew 14: 22-33

When in Doubt

The college student sat with his mother in the surgery waiting room. He was anxious and he willingly said so.

"How are you feeling?" I asked him.

"Not too good," he said. "Scared."

He knew his knee would heal slowly. But worse, he was afraid he's never wake up from the anesthetic. He felt like he might cry.

"Should we have a prayer together?" I asked him.

"You can have one for the two of you," he said. So I prayed with his mother, relatively certain he was listening. He survived the surgery, and he's hobbling all over town these days, relieved.

When I suggested we pray, the young man felt an internal resistance to faith which many of us have experienced. Sometimes we can't seem to let go and trust God. We hate to trust something unseen and unscientific. We resist expressions of faith. Prayer is so, so *vague*. Singing a hymn in church seems like a commitment somehow. It's embarrassing. We aren't sure what people will think of us when we pray out loud. We resist taking risks. We rationalize. We let doubt overcome us.

It's easy to understand why we distance ourselves from faith. In recent centuries, the western world has chosen to trust something else: the scientific method. We rely on logic and the visible, we demand proof. We are people of the modern mind. We trust the tangible, the known. That day before surgery, the college student wasn't certain the unseen God was available. It was a hard moment for him, because he wasn't all that sure that the human surgeon and human anesthetist were reliable either. He hated feeling vulnerable and praying only magnified his sense of vulnerability. He felt like he was in over his head.

Well, he was in good company. Peter was also in over his head in our gospel text today. It was 3:00 a.m. and the waters of the sea were rough. He was jostled awake in the night. Peter was a seasoned fisherman, accustomed to an unsettled sea, but the wind was against them and the waves beat on the boat. A spray of water smacked his face with cold. Then one of the disciples pointed to a figure out on the water. It was Jesus. He was coming to them. Some of them were scared - "It's a ghost" But Jesus reassured them. "Take heart, it is I; have no fear."

Peter was thrilled! That was Jesus! Peter was often such an impetuous man - outspoken, quick to express his emotions. "Lord, if it is you, bid me come to you on the water." And Jesus said, "Come." Enthusiastically, Peter clamored over the side of the boat onto the rough waters. He kept his gaze straight ahead on Jesus. He didn't pay attention to the white caps on the rolling waves. He ignored the wind. Peter knew where he was headed and moved forward.

Then something happened. Peter lost his focus. He began to feel the wind stinging his rough cheeks. The waves distracted him. He suddenly knew: he was out on the sea, over his head. People don't walk on water! He doubted Jesus. He doubted himself. He began to sink. "Lord, save me!" Jesus immediately reached out his hand and caught him, saying, "O you of little faith, why did you doubt?"

Indeed. Why *do* we doubt? Why do many of us hold back, afraid to trust? Why do we insist on feeling miserable and frightened in the midst of life's storms, rather than reaching out to Jesus, to God? Why do we tighten up our stomach and upper arms, steel our eyes against emotions and avoid saying or singing our faith, especially in public? What holds us back?

We resist because we're human. Human beings hate to feel or to acknowledge vulnerability. We'd much rather pretend that science has all the answers than admit that we are earthlings, subject to the powers of the wind and sea and God. We often fail to recognize that when we're in a storm, we have an opportunity to get closer to God. We prefer to act confident, even if it's false confidence, even when we're scared that we won't wake up from surgery. Human beings hate vulnerability because it leaves us out in storms, over our heads, altogether mortal and alone. We are like quaking bunny rabbits, sitting paralyzed with fear, vulnerable to the wolf and winter. Creatures.

Peter overcame his doubt and fear - at least for a while. He climbed out onto the sea and as long as he kept his focus on Jesus where real power resided, he was on top of it all. Peter knew he was just a person, a creature, so he depended on Jesus. As long as he did that, he walked forward, because Jesus was there, supporting him.

When Peter lost his focus, he became afraid and began to sink. He no longer relied on Jesus, but began to expect *himself* to be capable of this great feat and self-sufficiency. He would have perished in deep water had he not acknowledged vulnerability and cried out for help. Finally, rather than attempt to entirely manage his situation independently, he cried out, "Lord save me!"

So it is with us. Often we expect ourselves to be self-sufficient, independent. We do not acknowledge our vulnerability, we do not cry out for help. Our culture (and our human nature) tells us, "You don't need help. You don't need God. You have nuclear weapons. You have the Mayo Clinic. You have actuarial tables. You have the support of your colleagues. You don't need God. You can beat back the waves of your life. You're not really vulnerable. You're pretty darned capable!"

Armed with such illusions, we go out onto the sea, naive and optimistic, covering our vulnerability and with very little spiritual focus. We come to church, but we take no emotional risks. We do not risk saying or thinking we need God - it feels too vulnerable, too out of control. We do not pray aloud because it implies that we believe, that we need help. We are distracted by life's empty promises of material comfort and self-sufficiency, and before we know it, we're in over our heads.

There is a passage in Hebrews which says, "Now faith is the assurance of things hoped for, the conviction of things not seen." *Not* seen. The scientific method cannot draw us a picture of God. The surgeon cannot guarantee success. Material comforts do not provide unequivocal security. What I'm saying is that all of life is a risk. Faith takes risks without guarantees. Doubt creeps in and whispers, "Prove it. Show me." Faith simply replies, "Faith is not provable. It is, by definition, not reliant on the visible." Our lesson today is drawing us away from a logical, concrete perspective, to one of risk-taking. Believers hop over the side of the boat, and dare to speak despite doubt.

It used to bother me greatly to pray out loud. Sometimes I felt like a hypocrite, sometimes I just felt inadequate. At some level, though, I think I was afraid that if I said something faithful out loud, I'd have to turn over my control of life to God. I would be visibly vulnerable. No way. I didn't want to do that. I wasn't sure enough about God to dare to pray aloud. But my pastor encouraged me. "Just say it, Judie. Just do it. Don't worry about your ability. Don't worry about your doubt." It was a lot like the swimming coach who used to say, "Just do it. Just try diving in."

Finally I did it. I took the risk. I spoke the words. I prayed aloud, once, many times. And then, wonder! I realized I believed what I had said! The words took on faith for me. God had been there all the time and was activated. I dived in and I was swimming. It worked!

One doesn't necessarily get faith first and then act. One

doesn't feel sure and confident and then believe. Quite the opposite. We often act in spite of unbelief. We don't have to fake confidence. Rather, we acknowledge our vulnerability and need, and say, "Lord, help me." That's when God enters in - when we leave the door open a crack. It may not feel comfortable, especially at first. But being human, if we're honest, isn't very comfortable at times.

There are no assurances in life. The good may die young, a job may be pulled from beneath us, surgery is scary and a storm blows up on the lake. Our logic and science may assist us, but they will not save us. Faith seems like a risk. But life is a risk. There are no guarantees. We *are* vulnerable because we're human. What we do have are the promises throughout scripture that we are in God's care.

When you see Jesus coming toward you, be drawn by God's power over the side of the boat. Doubt and storms are opportunities to get closer to God. If you get scared or doubtful, just call out for help. Jesus will be there to keep your head above water. Keep your spiritual focus on the unseen and move forward. The wind will cease and the peace of God which passes all understanding will keep and guard your hearts in Christ Jesus, our
living Lord.

Drawing by Susan Friesen

The Rev. Judith M. Mattison
Mount Olivet Lutheran Church, Minneapolis
Christmas Day, 1987

The Touch of Christmas

Sometime in Mid-December
she looked around the house and thought
I simply have to dress things up a bit;
only a few days left now.
And so she put pine boughs along the mantle,
and a fragrant candle on the small table
that her grandfather had lovingly made
in his workshop many years before.
In the window, a lighted wreath.
On the table, a bowl of holly and
in the corner of the darkened room,
a small creche -
angels, shepherds, cattle, sheep
and a family of Middle Eastern people;
Mary, Joseph and a small baby, whose name was Jesus.
A touch of Christmas throughout her home.
It looked lovely.
It felt good.
The tree would come later
after the family arrived home for their annual visit.
For now, it was these small things
that made Christmas real.
The Touch of Christmas,
conveyed in candles and holly and lights,
in the presence of the branches
which were ever-green.

The woman was like us.
She liked to have the Touch of Christmas in her life.
All the rest of the weary year

we wait, even without knowing it,
for the moment when we will be touched by
the Spirit of God
the Spirit of God-with-us,
the Spirit of Christ's mass;
which we often casually toss off
as the Christmas Spirit.

All year long we wait
even without knowing it
for moments when we sense that God
actually cares enough about us,
and about this world in which we find ourselves
that God would choose to be among us.
We long to believe that God wants us
and loves us
and trusts us
and will forgive us,
no matter how casually
we toss off the Christmas Spirit.
As we walk the weary road
we yearn to hear the angels sing.

And sometimes they do -
in the middle of July or October.
Angels sing as one of us reaches beyond our cynicism
and touches the life of one who needs us.
In the heat of August or the dreariness of March
God is with us.
The Spirit of Christmas comes
when we give up our fear of doing without
and give from ourselves that which we
would prefer to keep -
which is often in the form of dollar bills
or shared power.
We know that when we open our fists

and share that which we claim
we have earned and deserve to keep -
it is the Spirit of Christmas
which has generated that generosity.
As soon as we let go and give
we know - we have been touched with Christmas.
Even in March or August or May.

Even in the darkness and cold of January,
the trees are ever-green,
reminding us that God is ever-present
    ever-available
    ever-living.
God is more than our expectations of life.
God is reliable,
even when we don't understand
and can scarcely believe
that there is meaning to all of what happens.
The ever-green, ever-living God
comes to us with the Touch of Christmas
daily.
The bells of Christmas chime once more
when someone says,
Hold on. God is coming to help you.
Don't give up, my friend.
God is ever-available, ever-present,
ever-loving
ever-good.

As we walk through the echoing rooms
of the house of our personal inner life,
we long to dress it up a bit.
But we know that we cannot do it.
We can be sometimes cheerful
    and that is good.
We can be sometimes generous

and the angels sing.
We can be sometimes loving
    and the world is eased from its tension.
But we cannot be ever-green.
We are human beings
and we cannot be always confident
or generous or kind.
Even on Christ's mass day
we will quarrel or find fault,
and we will hate ourselves
for our imperfection.
We cannot dress up our lives
with a few boughs of gentleness
and an ornament of good will.
For our will is weak
and our habits are harmful.
We cannot be Christmas every day
because we are only children who fail.
We can only come to the creche,
    the manger
    the cave
and see the Christ Child
and let God come to us -
in March or January,
in June or December.
God finds the way to touch us
with the Spirit of love and sacrifice.

We can leave here today
knowing that we are the Touch of Christmas
in others' lives,
because God came to be among us,
because God was that baby Jesus
and loved us in spite of ourselves.
Because our God is so generous and caring,
we can be the Touch of Christmas.

We will wrap our wreath of love
around the shoulders of those
who scarcely believe they are loveable.
We will be friends to those who need us
and we will be ever-available to them,
    even when they flail against our love
    or drive us away in fear
    or disappoint us by being selfish.
It won't be us, loving them in spite of themselves.
It will be God-in-us.
It will be Christmas in us.

When the world says, Fight,
God-in-us will say Wait...Love!
When the world weeps with famine or despair,
God-with-us will say
I'm here. I'll try to help.
I won't forget
even in April or November or May.
We will not only brush the world
with a momentary gift of good intentions,
but we will roll up our sleeves like grown-up people
and serve the world
because that's what the grown-up baby did -
the baby become Teacher,
Jesus the healer,
Jesus the crucified,
Jesus the Son of the Most High.
The Touch of Christmas
was not wistful nor sentimental.
The Touch of Christmas
was God-with-us in honest, confrontive
yet loving and enduring ways.
The Touch of Christmas lights up
the lonely corners of a dreary world
and the darkest corners of our hidden hearts.

It is the inspired acts of people
who are touched by God
which makes Christmas real.
This is more than dressing up in December.
This is fragrant Light,
    not of candles
    or wreathes
    or trees -
This is the fragrant Light of the Everlasting,
burning in our hearts throughout the year.
The people who walked in darkness
have seen a great light;
those who dwelt in a land of deep darkness
on them has light shined.
For to us a child is born.
God has come to us forever.
And we are touched by an everlasting love
which will never let us go - ever.
The Touch of Christmas is ours
to have
and to give.

Reverend Barbara E. Mraz

The Rev. Barbara E. Mraz

Born: St. Paul, Minnesota
Religious Background: Episcopal; raised Lutheran
Education: B.A. With Honors, Speech and Public Address,
M.A. in Education, Univ. of Mn..; Diaconal Study
Program, Episcopal Diocese of Minnesota, Minneapolis,
ordained January 25, 1982.
Employment: deacon, St. David's Episcopal Church
(preaching, adult education); also currently teaching
Women's Studies and Communications at The Blake
School; formerly deacon at St. John's Episcopal Church,
Minneapolis.
Personal: married to Steve Bougie, quality assurance
manager;daughters Anna, seventeen, and Emily, fifteen
Hobbies and Interests: freelance speaking and writing
(contributor to *Star-Tribune, Minnesota Women's Press*);
reading, gardening, movies, women's history and
literature, antiques, historic houses, how the past informs
the present.

Feminist theologians say that women's spirituality is
rooted in the concrete, the particular, the "dailyness of
life." Appropriately, what I remember most clearly about
many of the great occasions of my life is what I wore.

I stepped up to the microphone, the red and green
plaid taffeta skirt on my new dress crinkling as I walked.
My patent leather shoes gleamed beneath snow-white
anklets and a gigantic red bow held my dark curled hair
back from my face. I had never been this dressed up before.

My grandma had outfitted me for this, my first
Christmas pageant. Taking my turn in a line of children, I
was going to recite two lines about wise men "coming from
afar." Nervously and in a soft, tentative voice, I would
"speak my piece," as we called it. I was five years old.

Although the path to the pulpit has been anything but
straight, "speaking my piece" has defined my subsequent

life in the church.

Raised in the conservative Wisconsin Synod of the Lutheran church, my early life in the church was marked by Sunday School classes with Bible verses to memorize, movies depicting Bible stories that were low-budget versions of "Ben Hur," and for the truly faithful, gold stars placed on the attendance chart on the wall. Two years of twice-a-week Confirmation classes in seventh and eighth grade culminated in Confirmation Sunday, the first time most of the girls wore "heels" and corsages. We had memorized Luther's *Small Catechism*, including the sections entitled "What Does This Mean?" that followed each major doctrine. At that point in our lives, it was our job to memorize meanings, not debate them. Challenging authority.of any kind was not uppermost in our minds.

As much fun as I had in the church, as much as I learned there, and as drawn as I was to the sense of community, ritual and celebration I experienced there, never once did it occur to me to make the church my life's work. Wonderful female Sunday School teachers were my role models, but that was it. Women were not allowed to be on the church vestry or hold leadership positions of any kind. I certainly had never seen or even heard of a clergy*woman*.

Following high school, my doubts about Christianity grew, young-adult cynicism arrived on schedule, and I moved from St. Paul to Minneapolis. I also moved out of the ranks of churchgoers. Sunday mornings became time for leisurely newspaper reading and brunches with friends. This was the pattern for ten years.

What brought me back was the experience of parenthood. I felt guilty about not having my babies baptized. (Guilt is an emotion that has periodically served me well.) I also had been unable to replace the sense of community the church had always given me, and was ready again to look at some of life's tougher questions. So, wearing the ankle-length Indian print skirt, peasant top, sandals and large hoop earrings that characterized my life in the mid-seventies, I checked out the local Episcopal church because my sister-in-law went there.

Within six years I had become a member of that church, served on the Vestry and as senior warden, become a lay reader and entered the ordained ministry,

I was obviously ready to come back.

What drew me more than anything was that this newly-found church spoke to my mind as well as to my heart, that intellect was seen as a companion to faith, not its enemy. As much as I longed for the community and ritual that the church offered, a thinking, questioning atmosphere was an absolute prerequisite for any religion to be acceptable to me. The Episcopal church offered this to me, on my terms. In my favorite series of children's books, Maud Hart Lovelace's Betsy-Tacy stories, Betsy tells her Baptist father that she loves the Episcopal church because "the liturgy is like a poem." She says that she was "just born to be an Episcopalian." Me, too.

I joined the Episcopal church in 1975. The next year the church voted to ordain women. A good sign, I thought.

From the start, my "call" to ministry has been a call to preach. Maybe it is a more specific call than that experienced by most people who become ordained. But preaching is my vocation, my spirituality, and the passion of my heart. It is something that I have been led into with preparations that took place well before I knew where they would lead. And then I was ordained and put on the deacon's stole and long, white clerical vestments. I was so used to seeing male clergy in these outfits that I wondered how I could make the ensemble more "feminine" - even though it was already virtually a dress!

It is a tremendous responsibility to mount the stairs to the pulpit and interpret what you believe to be *the word of God*. Sometimes as I walk there, I ask myself what in the world I think I'm doing - who do I think I am anyway - a divorced, remarried, ex-Lutheran female in clerical vestments, make-up, and large earrings. For I have been unwilling to sacrifice part of my femaleness for this role. It has been an extra gift to hear women tell me what seeing those earrings in the pulpit has meant to them.

Those strong, confident, male German Lutheran pastors of my youth who seemed to have all the answers loom in my memory, taller and more imposing than ever. Perhaps that is why I have never felt "worthy" to be in the ministry. I have worried that I can be morally ambivalent, that my faith is shakable, that I am too self-centered to be "clergy." But awhile ago I stopped arguing the point with myself and now offer what I have. This has been a joy and a privilege.

Perhaps the greatest gift I bring to the ministry is my skepticism, the fact that I am always struggling. More than anyone, I identify with those for whom faith is not easy. Now it is mainly for them - us - that I speak my piece.

The Rev. Barbara Mraz
St. David's Episcopal Church, Minnetonka
December 30, 1988
John 1:1-18

What I Learned from the Rabbi

*"In the beginning was the Word, and the
Word was with God, and the Word was God."* John 1:1

I drove along Minnehaha Parkway to St. Paul,
wondering if I was doing the right thing.

I arrived at Temple of Aaron on the West River Road
and saw the large sign on the lawn - "Help Save Soviet
Jews" - in lettering that resembled barbed wire - and was
momentarily jolted by the sign's intensity, and also by
doubts about what I as a Christian was about to do. But
somehow I knew that it was going to be worth it. For the
next six Tuesday nights I had signed up to hear Rabbi
Bernard Raskas, senior rabbi of this large Jewish
congregation, talk about Jesus.

Exploring a faith other than our own is at once a
seductive and frightening experience. Seductive, because
this other faith may hold answers that our own does not.
Frightening, because our own faith may be so fragile, and
our commitment to it so tentative, that we fear it won't be
able to stand up to the intellectual assaults of another
philosophy. Maybe there are some things we're better off
not knowing?

I felt all of this as I walked through the heavy, carved,
wooden doors of the synagogue. Would my Christianity be
shaken here? Would I learn that Jesus wasn't the Messiah?
Wasn't God?

Inside the building, many things were familiar and
comforting: the reassuring feeling of being in a place of
worship with pews, pulpit and prayer books; the large gold

inscriptions over the sanctuary door - "The Lord is my shepherd" and "Into thy hands I commend my spirit" (the realization striking home that these phrases must be from the "Old Testament" or Hebrew Scriptures, and not only Gospel references to Jesus), and the expectant look, the hunger for answers, on the faces of the people assembled there. Several hundred people, Christians *and* Jews, had been intrigued by the promise that tonight Rabbi Raskas would be talking about the first century and his views on Jesus. It was an overflow crowd.

As I looked around the large, star-shaped sanctuary at Temple of Aaron with its plush, padded seats and radiant red and gold flame-emblazoned curtain at the front of the room, I also felt the strange absence of something familiar. I realized that what was missing was the insignia of Christianity - there were no Crosses, no Baptismal font, no stained-glass saints. The synagogue felt incomplete and alien in that respect, though I knew that God was worshiped here.

It was not until the end of the six weeks that I realized that Jesus would have loved this place; he would have felt at home with the Hebrew Scriptures, the rabbinic references, the scholarly dialogue and the ancient prayers. Jesus, I remembered with a start, was a Jew, not a Christian.

My visits to Temple of Aaron left the issue of different faiths very much in my mind and raised the question of "true religion" - What is it? Who has it? How do all the faiths of the world fit together? Can they all be right? How can you tell?

Today's sermon will examine some of these complex theological issues from one particular perspective. Today I'd like to tell you what I learned from the rabbi about Jesus - and how it affected my Christianity.

Rabbi Raskas is in his sixties, typically attired in suit, tie and yarmulke, witty, learned, a scholar and, I am sure, a liberal. (One lecture is dedicated to the memory of Hubert Humphrey, obviously a personal friend - "I *pine* for that man," says the rabbi.) The rabbi is also intensely American. Referring to the Nazi march across Poland, he tells us, "I know where I'd be if my mother had missed the boat to America: buried in a pit somewhere in Poland. I *know* what I owe America." To someone of my Vietnam-stained generation, such unabashed patriotism is, in itself, a curiosity.

Most of what I learned in this class was about Jesus, the background and basis for many of his teachings, and also details about first-century Jewish life. It *was* an education, not only what I learned from the rabbi, but the thinking that it forced me to do about my faith.

In spite of being an ordained person, often I am not someone who wears her Christianity easily, like a comfortable old sweater or well-worn jeans. Rather I wear it self-consciously, sometimes awkwardly, more like a jacket that I've had for a long time but can never get totally used to. It fits and wears well, but I am always aware that many people in the world have on a jacket that is far different from mine. While "God" is not a problem for me, I still struggle with Jesus Christ and how he fits into the panorama of world religions and the daily struggles of my own life.

Like the twelve Apostles, like the early Christians, and like the apostle Paul, Jesus was Jewish. From the rabbi I learned that Jesus was *very* Jewish, his teaching universally rooted in Jewish tradition. It was only in discussing himself and his ministry that Jesus diverted from traditional Judaism. I was not upset or disappointed to find that most of Jesus' teachings were not "original" - instead the realization that Jesus was firmly rooted in his Judaism was somehow reassuring.

Some time ago I concluded that religion is mainly about *revelation*; that it is a study of how God is revealed to us. Rabbi Raskas also talked about revelation, and told us that he considers Christianity *a way* of God spreading His truth to the world. To be a Jew, he said, is difficult. It involves circumcision, dietary restrictions and study of the Law; Judaism is not interested in evangelism and converts. But Christianity, he said, is accessible to anyone; it travels lightly, without many of the legalistic trappings of Judaism; it is perhaps more universal in scope and has a sense of mission. The rabbi felt that Christianity was more suited to reaching the people of first-century Palestine and Europe than Judaism was. This is not to say that we should all be Christians and not Jews; it is to say that God can be revealed in more than one way.

This is a very troubling idea for many Christian fundamentalists. There is a Bible verse that is quoted to "prove" that only Christians will be "saved: "Jesus said, 'I am the Way, the Truth, and the Life. No one comes to the Father but by me" (John 14:6). Although I have debated the language of this many times with fundamentalist friends, I remain unconvinced that those millions in the world, past, present and future, who have not "accepted" Jesus (or ever heard of him) will be punished everlastingly by a loving God.

The Roman Catholic priest Andrew Greeley provides an interesting analysis. In *The Jesus Myth*, Greely observes that if life exists on other planets in the universe, as it well may, how can the earthly, first-century historical figure of Jesus "save" whatever forms of life exist there? Jesus lived in a particular time and place. Does the Jesus of the Gospels "trod the galaxies?" Greeley wonders. Or would God have to be incarnated in another, culturally appropriate form? Thinking in cosmic dimensions about Jesus Christ, about the potential of "alien Gospels," is a powerful challenge to Biblical literalism.

The Gospel assigned for today gives one perspective on this issue. The first verses of the poetic, beautiful, and controversial Book of John are among my favorite verses in the Bible: "In the beginning was the Word, and the Word was with God and the Word was God." John goes on, "And the Word became flesh and dwelt among us, full of grace and truth" (John 1:14). John's main description of Jesus is *the Word*. These verses, more than any other, in my opinion, shed light on the nature of Jesus.

Though other forms of communication exist, words are primary. Words express our innermost thoughts and feelings; they reveal who we are. Jesus is God's *word* - his communication to us. Jesus says, "He who has seen me has seen the Father" (John 14:9). John says that the historical person of Jesus communicates the *nature* of God.

But words are limited and imperfect communicators; the same word means different things to different people. Meaning is tied to specific times and places. And Jesus has been interpreted in hundreds of ways, from insignificant teacher to God of Gods.

Going further, the same word can be translated into many languages. Here the possibilities are endless. Perhaps God's Word - his expression of Himself - is translated into a different form for a Buddhist or Muslim than it is for me. I've never been comfortable with a hardline, Bible-thumping Christianity that dismisses as wrong the religious beliefs of two-thirds or more of the world's population. John's discussion of "the Word" is suitably inclusive. Put another way, we all perceive the same Light, though we may see it through different panes of glass.

While there is tremendous comfort in the idea of a universal God that is bigger than any specific faith, there is also the need for a personal God that we know and understand. The rabbi tells the story of the five-year-old boy who was at the State Fair and got separated from his family. He stood in the middle of the Midway and called, "Sarah, Sarah, Sarah!" When his mother ran up to him, she put her arms around him and asked, "Why didn't you just call for *Mommy*?" And he said, "I don't want *any* mommy. I want *mine*."

And I have realized that, although I honor their visions, I don't want any religion. I want mine.

In these days of "bottom line" thinking, the bottom line is that Jesus is the way that God has revealed him/herself *to me*. This is true for many reasons. One is that I see the major themes in the life of Christ as the power of love and the certainty of renewal and resurrection, and this is how I have experienced life again and again. Christianity resonates with my own experience and so I trust it.

The last night our class met at the synagogue was last Tuesday, election night. It was also the night before *Kristellnacht*, "The Night of Broken Glass," the official beginning of the Holocaust when, in 1938, Hitler's soldiers stormed through Germany, burning synagogues, smashing Jewish shop windows, and arresting, killing and deporting thousands of Jews.

The rabbi reminded us of this solemn occasion and reflected, "You know, here we are in this room tonight, fifty years later, Jews and Christians studying together, and next door people are voting for the president of the United States. Hitler didn't win and there's a lesson in that." And for me, I thought, the lesson is the same as the Cross and the Resurrection: suffering and death are defeated; life is renewed.

I accept Christianity as a gift that has been given to me. It is my family heritage, my birthright, my tradition, and I claim it as my own. In a way, I'm amazed that I'm still here in the church at all, especially after the cynicism of my adolescence and the skepticism and disbelief that accompanied a ten-year absence from the church. Initially, I returned only because my conscience wouldn't let up on me until I had my children baptized somewhere. By accident, I came to an Episcopal church and I stayed.

Ultimately, I couldn't reject the heritage. Perhaps in my case, as in yours, our Baptisms "took" and we are "marked as Christ's own forever." To concur with Martin Luther: "Here I stand. God help me. I can do no other."

Objectivity is not really possible in the realm of faith. There are no "primary sources" about Jesus, no autobiography, no letters, no papers. Scripture records only those observations of faithful disciples who loved him and believed in him. But the eyes of faith are to be trusted no less than the eyes of doubt.

History, heritage, and traditions are to be studied in earnest. But ultimately we are left, even after a lifetime of study and reflection, skeptics and scholars alike, to set down our books, put aside our questions, quiet our frantic hearts, and bow before the mystery.

More than anything, *that* is what I learned from the rabbi.

Drawing by Susan Friesen

The Rev. Barbara Mraz
St. David's Episcopal Church, Minnetonka
June 24, 1990
Matthew 10:16-33

(Reprinted from the Minneapolis *Star-Tribune*, June 11, 1990)

Soviet Sister

These are exciting times for those of us who lived through the Fifties and Sixties. We are the generation of children who learned to dive under our school desks and cover our heads in the event of Russian nuclear attack, and saw our neighbors stocking backyard bomb shelters with canned goods.

So today it seems that the impossible is happening as the Berlin Wall comes down, democracy gains strength in Eastern Europe, and the leader of the Soviet Union causes traffic jams on a visit to Minneapolis. *Glasnost*, "the new openness" decreed by President Gorbachev, has pulled back the "Iron Curtain," shed a brighter light on the countries behind it, and shown us that the people there are potential allies - even friends, if we can navigate through our differences and somehow make the connection.

Today's Gospel from Matthew strikes an amazingly contemporary note with its emphasis on reconciliation, risk-taking, and the relationship between the two. Jesus tells us to be less skeptical, less cautious about approaching each other: "Do not worry about what you are to say. When the time comes, the words you need will be given you. For it is not you who will be speaking; it is the Spirit of your Father speaking in you." This is a powerful admonition for those of us who feel we need a script for every occasion and cannot act without a plan.

I am basically an introvert. Frequently, I like to work alone, to have time to reflect and plan. Too often this turns into an unwillingness to reach out to other people, so that I can remain on my own timetable and conserve my energy for my own projects. It be-comes more than typical "Minnesota reticence."

My caution and skepticism may be extreme, but it is representative of a tendency in all of us to embrace the familiar, to have the friends we've always had, and to do it the way we've always done it. There is also some insecurity reflected in this attitude, that if we don't have a plan ready in a new situation, maybe we will be unable to function spontaneously. We will be tongue-tied, inappropriate, or otherwise disfunctional. Not only does the Gospel tell us that "the words we need will be given us," but this restrictive mindset is one that is doomed in the global village that is the world in the Nineties.

We learn the necessity and rewards of risk-taking and reaching out in various ways at different times in life. I had to re-learn it again this spring as life sneaked up on me, disarmed my defense system, and forever altered my perceptions and sensibilities. It was because of Tanya.

There is a continuous parade of international visitors through the high school where I work, exchange students, delegations of foreign visitors, a teacher or administrator or two. Last fall we had a delegation of thirty students and teachers from Denmark visit us for a month. I didn't pay much attention to them because I was preoccupied and just didn't get to it. Anyway, more Scandinavians in Minnesota - there was no mystique here that seemed worth disrupting my already busy schedule.

So this spring when Chuck Ritchie, the Russian language teacher, approached me to see if I would host a visiting Soviet teacher/administrator in my Women's Studies class, I sighed inwardly and thought that here I was again being asked to commit to some predictable "So what is it like in your country?" discussions with troublesome accents, forced smiles, and interest that seems more pretend than real. But Chuck had me cornered so I told him that sure, "Tanya" could come to class, I guess.

Tanya showed up the first day in my Communications class; she listened politely to my students' speeches and talked informally about her city of Novasibirsk and her impressions of America. I asked her what had surprised her the most. "The fact that Americans do not seem sincerely interested in us. They smile and say hello, not much more," she said in a melodic voice with exquisite English pronunciation. "It's very important people in the Soviet Union right now to feel that Americans care about them."

I had no response, because in a few sentences this attractive, thirty-seven-old foreign visitor had given an accurate summary of my carefully-concealed indifference, my poorly-masked arrogance, and appalling ethnocentrism. I was unsettled, to say the least.

The next day in my Women's Studies class Tanya watched a film with us about weight and self-esteem in women and I asked her if Soviet women are as obsessed with thinness and appearance as Americans are. And the barrage began.

Tanya talked nonstop for twenty minutes about how she worries about her weight every day of her life, how hard it is to diet with the shortage of fruits and vegetables, various diets that she and her friends have tried, the problem of cooking too much food for holiday celebrations and having to use it up, the strategy of not eating lunch. And as Tanya and I talked, the cultural barriers evaporated, we laughed a lot, finished each other's sentences, and almost forgot about the fifteen female students sitting there, puzzled. My defenses had been broken down by a Soviet from Siberia talking about diets.

Tentatively, I asked Tanya if she would be free to come to my house for dinner the next night and meet some more American women. She said yes. Eagerly.

The dinner was a revelation. Tanya arrived and immediately brought out two red and black enameled boxes. She held my arm with touching formality and said, "These are for you, Bar-bar-a," giving my name the three syllables that it's supposed to have and is never given. Good grief, this was making me teary-eyed...

Tanya had told me that she, her teen-age son and her husband live in a medium-size apartment, and as she looked around my large, lace-curtained living room she quietly sighed, "Oh..." a soft expression she would use often when a more intense reaction seemed inappropriate, a tender and purposely-restrained amazement. It was echoed another time when she saw the cheap prices of shoes on a sale rack at a discount store. "This cannot be," she said almost to herself. It made my heart ache.

We could have all sat for days at the dinner table. The four women I had invited and I barraged Tanya with questions. We were no longer making polite inquiries, we were passionately interested, the six of us sitting there in south Minneapolis, only a half a block away from the Watson home where Raisa Gorbachev would visit some six weeks later.

We asked Tanya about her family, her job, her education, shopping, vacations, food and cooking, birth control, childbirth, medical care, dentistry, money, politics. Tanya told us about the long lines, the shortages of all types of goods in the shops, and the fact that winter boots cannot be bought with less than a month's wages. Tanya's mother stands in the food lines while Tanya and her sister are at work. "My mother gets a bag for each of our three families. It saves me a lot of time," Tanya explained. She said that there are many beautiful women in the Soviet Union but "the deprivation - it does something to them that is very sad." She was amazed at the array of convenience foods and microwavable products in America. "If I lived here," she said, "I don't think I would ever cook." We laughed. "We don't!"

I saw Tanya two or three more times before she left.

She was very busy. In addition to teaching in the school Russian program, in the course of a week she visited a Native American sweat lodge ("a deeply spiritual experience," she said), a psychic, and a holistic healer. I'd never done any of these things and I envied her daring spirit.

One day the two of us went out to lunch and talked about love, marriage, husbands and our children. We talked about our affinity for "manly men," about the many shades and hues of marriage, and about the pain of leaving friends.

Knowing she was to leave soon, I wanted to get Tanya some gifts. Once I began shopping, I was seized with an overpowering urge to buy her everything I could think of. I wanted to buy her clothes, shoes, jewelry, cosmetics, books, household items, anything to make her life easier and that she would enjoy. I found myself wanting to spend hundreds of dollars before I stopped myself. For it wasn't just affection for Tanya that was driving me. It was a deep feeling of injustice at the core of my being that was inflaming my judgment. And I, who consider my United Way contribution so carefully, balancing it against my own family's "needs," who is impatient with yet another request from the Heart Fund, now I wanted to make up for it, to share my appallingly vast resources, to make a feeble attempt to even the score.

But no amount of short-term buying I could do for Tanya was going to remedy the inequities. I could not play the sophisticated older sister, showering the younger, less fortunate sibling with extravagance for the fun of seeing her reaction. And I did not want Tanya's pride and dignity to suffer from my cultural guilt.

I settled for an engraved silver picture frame - "To Tanya, in friendship." In it I put a picture of the two of us, smiling, arms around each other's waists. I also bought two bottles of Tea Rose perfume, one for her and one for me. It made me feel good knowing we would be smelling the same roses.

Struggling with Tanya's departure and how much I missed her, I asked Chuck, "Is Tanya a typical Russian?" "Yes and no," he said. "I certainly can't imagine a better representative of the Soviet Union. Maybe you want to go over there and find out?" "Oh no, I couldn't...really...I'm not real...brave." Earlier I had made the same observation to Tanya, when she suggested that I visit her in Siberia. "Well, Bar-bar-a, it may be time now to become brave," she said.

In this most unexpected of encounters, in this profound relationship that I was shamed into accepting, the words that I needed *were* given me. I did not need a script; I did not have a plan. The words were given me and friendship took over from there. The Spirit of love took me by the hand, overcame my reticence and my busyness, and insisted that I see the world and my own priorities in a different light. And I saw that the words in the Gospel to reach out to each other in love, without fear, are not only an admonition to us, they are also a gift.

When I had asked with typical Scandinavian reticence if it would be all right with Tanya if I took her to lunch, her response had been as unrestrained and exuberant as my request had been cautious: "Yes, Bar-bar-a! That would be more than all right!"

Dear Tanya, Soviet sister, soul-mate from half a world away, next time I will be less judgmental, less preoccupied, more brave. Your arms outstretched in friendship, your warmth, your intelligence and your spirit have changed me. And friendships like ours are changing the world. And that is "more than all right."

Susan S. Friesen

Her Women, as artist Susan S. Friesen describes her figurative work, recreate in a way only a female artist could, the existential anguish of being a woman. These paintings are strong, and direct in their impact and reveal the essential loneliness, fears, and vulnerability that comes with being a contemporary woman. The strength of these portraits, however, conveys the sense that these women have a rich inner life; they will survive and find fulfillment even in this imperfect world.

Susan Friesen was born in Niagara-On-The-Lake, Ontario, Canada and grew up on her family's fruit farm. She went to the University of Waterloo, Ontario on scholarship where she studied mathematics and computer science. In 1982 she graduated from the Ontario College of Art in Toronto in Communication and Design. Over the next two years she divided her time between figurative painting and textile design at the Toronto firm of Hamil Textiles. In 1984 she moved with her family to the Twin Cities where she has pursued her painting full time. Mother of three adult children, she lives in Gem Lake, Minnesota with her husband, Eric, and the friend appearing in the photograph below.

Drawing by Susan Friesen

Sacred Strands was set in Adobe Minion Display via
Microsoft Word for Windows on a LaserMaster
LM1000 printer at Lone Oak Press